CHOICES
DECISIONS THAT LAST A LIFETIME

TOM SAUNDERS

21ST CENTURY PRESS
PUBLISHING WITH PURPOSE

Copyright © 2003 *by Thomas C. Saunders Jr.*

Published by 21st Century Press

Springfield, MO 65807

All rights reserved. No part of this book may be used or reproduced in any manner whatsoever or stored in any database or retrieval system without written permission except in the case of brief quotations used in critical articles and reviews. All Scripture passages are from the *Life Application Study Bible*. (NIV) Tyndale House Publishers & Zondervan Publishing House. 1997.

Requests for permissions should be addressed to:
21st Century Press
2131 W. Republic Rd.
PMB 41
Springfield, MO 65807

ISBN 0-9728899-4-9

Cover: Lee Fredrickson
Book Design: Jeremy Montz and Terry White

Visit our web-site at: 21stcenturypress.com
                            and 21centurybooks.com
For childrens books visit: sonshippress.com
                            and sonshipbooks.com

DEDICATION

I would like to dedicate this work, first and foremost, to my Lord and Savior Jesus Christ. His love is a perfect love.

I would also like to acknowledge the many people that helped me refocus my life on Christ and those that walk with me everyday to keep me there. First of all I thank my beautiful wife Lauri. Her constant love, encouragement, and support sustain me everyday. Next are my wonderful children Chelsea, Alex, and Kori. They are my motivation to be more like Christ. I love them beyond words.

I want to thank my brothers and sisters in Christ that brought me back to Him. To Scott Teutsch, Don Francis, Karl and Loriann Kaufman, Craig Brooks, Ruth Workman and all my brothers and sisters at Eastwood Baptist Church. You not only directed me back to Jesus you gave me the strength to carry on through very difficult times. I praise God for all of you.

To Mike Warner, Barry Howe, Randy Kitchens, Nate Turner, Dan (Dr. Dano) Boyd, and all my brothers and sisters in Christ that served with me while at Kunsan Air Base, Korea. You taught, comforted, and supported me through my time in the "desert." Thank God you were all there.

To all my military brothers and sisters that served with me over 22 years in the United States Air Force, especially my family at Barksdale AFB, Louisiana, Robbie Watts, John Spronk, Dave Wyllie, Phil Semler, Shawn Dorsey, Doug Craighead, and Stan Barras. My God bless you all.

And finally to my family and friends, most of all, my

Grandpa, Ray Bradshaw. You are a wonderful Christian example and because of your quiet unselfish love, you brought many to Christ that might have otherwise spent an eternity separated from Him. Thank you for being my example and my grandpa.

TABLE OF CONTENTS

Introduction 7

Perspective 9

PART ONE
MY SPIRITUAL JOURNEY

1. A Spiritual Roller Coaster 15
2. Back In The Air Force And Church 27
3. It's Over 35
4. Father Really Does Know Best 45

PART TWO
UNDERSTANDING CHRISTIANITY

5. What Is A Christian? 67
6. The Character And Nature Of God 75
7. Religion Or Relationship 81

PART THREE
WHAT DOES GOD EXPECT FROM US

8. Be An Example 87
9. Judge Not 99
10. Mentoring A New Believer 105
11. Personal Responsibility 109
12. Finding The Answers 113

PART FOUR
TO BELIEVE OR NOT BELIEVE

13. Questions Or Excuses 119
14. Deception 125

PART FIVE
THE TOUGHEST ISSUES

15. Some Of Satan's Favorite Tactics 133
16. Sex And The Church 149
17. Conflict 155

PART SIX
CAN YOU BELIEVE IT?

18. God's Love 165
19. God Wants Me? 169

PART SEVEN
CLOSING THOUGHTS

Summary 179
Epilogue 183
Endnotes 187
Personal Profile 189

INTRODUCTION

Everyone has a story of how they came to Jesus Christ as their personal Lord and Savior; I'm no exception. Along the way I've learned a great deal about God and what He expects of me. I've also come to the conclusion that I was taught many things in the name of religion that were not in God's word: the Bible. This book is based partly on my experience as a leader, teacher, and counselor over the last twenty-five years and the lessons God taught me alone the way. This is a book about taking God out of the box that religion has put Him in and how religion is turning people away from Christ. It's also about where to find answers.

I want people to know that God provides us with all the information we need to answer any question or deal with any situation we face during our life in the Bible. And if we diligently search His word for those answers, He clearly reveals Himself to us. I want people to know that our Lord and Savior, Jesus of Nazareth is a loving, compassionate, and forgiving God. And though the Bible tells us He was a man of sorrows, Jesus had a great sense of humor. He loved to do the unpredictable and He loved to laugh. I want to challenge people to think outside the lines concerning their image of Jesus.

The Bible has a wealth of information, knowledge, and wisdom to offer us if we are willing to search its pages for direction. I'm excited about what the Lord is doing in my life and it is my pray that every Christian feel that same excitement. If not, why? Do you have God in a box; is the Bible a nuisance to read? Jesus came that we might have life and have it more abundantly; He leaves the choice to us to accept His offer.

PERSPECTIVE

My perspective of God has changed tremendously over the years. As a boy, I really had no understanding of who or what God was and I went to church on a sporadic basis. From time to time, I'd involve myself with the youth group until I became bored or found something better to do. I accepted Christ as my Savior at the age of 12 and followed in baptism on 28 February 1971. I believed what I professed, although I'm sure in retrospect, I didn't really understand what dedicating my life to Christ was all about.

I believe that when a person accepts Christ, they can never lose their salvation, however, as in the case of Charles Templeton, if they completely renounce and reject Jesus, the Bible is clear on this point. "Yet they rebelled and grieved his Holy Spirit. So he turned and became their enemy and he himself fought against them" (Isaiah 63:10). It also says, "The fool says in his heart, there is no God" (Psalm 14:1). These people, like Templeton, were probably never saved in the first place.

I first learned of Templeton while reading "The Case For Faith" by Lee Strobel. He tells of how Templeton went from preacher to agnostic because of **his** reasoning, much the same way Sigmund Freud tried to reason away faith. Both lived a life of futility. When I contemplate the great thinkers of history and their contributions to the human race, I always come back to the passage of scripture that reminds us that man's wisdom is foolishness in

9

the eyes of the Lord. Regardless of their brilliance, it amounts to nothing in God's eyes. Albert Einstein had the right idea when he said, "I want to know God's thoughts; the rest are details."

I'm also quite convinced that we can fall away from God to the point that we grieve and quench the Spirit and become so distant from the Lord that we can't hear His voice any longer. The Bible says, "And do not grieve the Holy Spirit of God, with whom you were sealed for the day of redemption" (Ephesians 4:30). That's not to say God left us or went in a different direction; we moved away from Him. I found this out in a very personal and painful way.

There were many contributing factors to my move away from God, but I can blame nobody but myself for the choices I made; some based on youthful arrogance, some because of ignorance, and some were just plain stupid. Unfortunately religion was one of those factors: not the church or the Bible but religion. (I'll discuss both choices and religion later in the book.) Now I'm as close to Christ as I've ever been in my life and religion had nothing to do with building my relationship with Christ. I've probably just lost much of the religious right with that statement but they're into religion. The Bible, Christian fellowship, mentors, research, love, and prayers turned my life around, not to mention the very painful pruning process the Lord uses to mold us into a more correct image of Christ. But isn't that what being a Christian is all about: being Christ-like? As I look back on my life, I can see how the Lord used the trials of life to teach and change me along the way. I know now that much of what I needed to know then was right in front of me in my Bible. I still have a long way to go and I look forward to what God

INTRODUCTION

has in store for me. I also know that the trip will be a little easier because I have a better understanding of God's will for my life and I know where to find answers when faced with difficult questions.

I suppose that when it gets right down to it, this is simply a personal testimony about how God continues to work in my life. My hope is that it may reach others and compel them to receive Jesus as their personal Lord and Savior. I have felt for years that I should write this book. Time and again, God continues to lay it on my heart to share what I've learned. I feel that I must follow His leading. If this is of my own volition then it will amount to nothing, but if it is from the Lord, it will reach those He intends it for. If one person is led to Him through this work, then it was worth every minute of time that I spent writing it.

My Spiritual Journey

1 A SPIRITUAL ROLLER COASTER

This account of my experience with the Lord sets the stage for the conclusions I draw in this book. As I mentioned earlier, my sometimes-tenuous relationship with the Lord started at a young age. My grandfather and my uncle were instrumental in my early spiritual life. They always encouraged me to attend church with them without forcing the issue. If I wanted to go, I called. If there were a special program they thought I'd like, they'd let me know about it and leave the choice to me.

I didn't realize it then, but they were teaching me one of my first lessons about winning others to Christ: plant the seed and let the Lord do the rest. I have seen so many people turned off to Christ by well-meaning, over-zealous people trying to stuff their beliefs down another's throat. Clubbing people over the head with the Bible or theology is not an effective way of leading others to Christ. I'll address this more in the chapter, Be An Example.

I was in and out of the youth group as a teen and looking back, I know my salvation was always secure because of my sincere faith that Christ died for my sins and that I was in need of His grace and mercy; what was lacking was a relationship with Him. So many Christians miss the greatest part about being a child of God because they are never taught or mentored in developing a relationship with God. They're lost in a religious shuffle and eventually end up falling away from God because, after the initial joy of accepting Christ as their savior, their life seems to be pretty much the way it was prior to asking Christ into their heart. But just as people aren't taught how to lead others to Christ, they also never learn how to be spiritual mentors. They remain babes in Christ. I will discuss the importance of mentoring believers later.

Another benefit of developing our relationship with Jesus is learning how to nurture our relationships with family and friends. Scripture addresses every aspect of relationship building imaginable including conflict management. How much better would our lives be if we knew more about resolving conflict instead of exacerbating it. The Bible makes it clear that we can't have a meaningful relationship with the Lord if we can't have meaningful relationships with those we deal with on a daily basis: families, friends, co-workers, congregants, and even strangers... "Therefore, if you are offering your gift at the altar and there remember that your brother has something against you, leave your gift there in front of the altar. First go and be reconciled to your brother; then come and offer your gift" (Matthew 5:23-24). Many times we forget that the only time a person may get to see and know Gods love is in how we treat them, stranger or not.

Air Force Bound

I bounced around in a few jobs after completing high school and joined the United States Air Force eight months after graduation. With no intentions of going to college, it seemed a logical and adventurous choice. At basic training in Texas, one of the favorite social activities was going to Sunday service. It was more than just an opportunity to get away from the rigors of the training; the services were contemporary services and in 1977 that was something new. Other than an opportunity to go downtown one time and to tour the base during the last week of training there wasn't much socializing other than church... technical training in Denver was quite a different story.

Any restoration of a relationship with God that began to blossom in Texas floundered once I got to Denver. After being told for six weeks when to do everything, including scratch ourselves, we were free to come and go as we pleased after in processing on the base. We did have a curfew but that was our only limitation and the drinking age was 19; a dangerous combination for several young men that felt they were just released from incarceration. Technical school was an eight-week party complete with drinking, fighting, carousing, discipline, and even a few discharges. God was the last thing anyone, including myself, was thinking about.

My on-again, off-again relationship with Jesus continued after my transfer to California to my first permanent duty station. Until my flight to Texas for basic training, I had never been on an airplane and other than a trip to Virginia when I was very young and a few excursions to Ohio, I had never been out of the state of Michigan; now I was living in California in the 1970's. Trouble wasn't hard to find. It was also my first experience with a church split.

There was a right crowd and a wrong crowd, spiritually speaking, when I arrived at my first squadron. The wrong crowd was pretty easy to find as it usually is in any situation. Keep in mind; I'm speaking strictly from a spiritual point of view here. Almost everyone in the squadron from the commander down to the lowest Airman, that would be me, was very dedicated to the Air Force and each other and humanly speaking were a pretty good group of men and women. But being young and being the 70's, the disco scene called and even a small town in California had several clubs to choose from.

That, combined with the recently ended Vietnam War and the attitude about casual marijuana use, made for lots of trouble if a person wasn't careful. I saw several promising young people lose out on a potentially great career because they got caught up in the drug scene. But as most self-serving satisfiers go, the party scene got old and after seeing what happen to a few people in my squadron, I didn't want to get entangled in something I would regret. Even though I wasn't as close to God as I should have been, He was still convicting me and trying to encourage me to see the light as it were.

It's funny how God puts everything we need right in front of use if we are only willing to search it out. It was no different in this situation. There was a group of devoted Christians in the squadron and as I felt the Lord's urging more and more, I sought them out. They quickly accepted me into their group and I immediately felt a sense of family that eluded me even before I left home. During this time, the church we attended went through a split; that sense of family slowly slipped away. I seemed to be in a spiritual abyss for the remaining time I was there but I believe it was there that I established my spiritual foundation, but it would be several years through much disappointment and heartache before I realized it.

A Rude Awakening

I was now on my way to Spain! Little did I know

what I was getting myself into by volunteering for this assignment. I had no idea if I would be back to the states before the end of my two-year assignment to Spain so I stopped off at home for a few weeks to spend some time with family and friends before my great adventure. The day after my return, my grandmother suffered a massive stroke, her body weakened from a long battle with diabetes she succumbed two days later on Mother's Day 1979. I remember the peace I felt at her funeral knowing that she was a child of God and she was now with the Lord and no longer suffering. Although many would miss her very much, we knew she was much better off now. Three weeks later I landed in Madrid Spain.

The flight to Spain was grueling to say the least. It started out with two flights and several military taxis before the 16-hour ride to Spain, yes 16 hours not including the time change. Before we got off the ground there was concern that because of head winds, passengers, and cargo they couldn't put enough fuel on the plane to make it to our first refueling stop in the Azores and still get off the ground. I didn't waste any time; I started to pray. We did make it to the Azores and then on to London. We did not deplane at either stop. The aircrew changed in London and as the new crew boarded the aircraft they filled the fuselage with spray deodorizer because of the stench from all of us packed into the plane for so long. After a stop at Rota Naval Station we landed at Torrejon Air Base outside of Madrid. We left the states about 7 PM Friday night. It was 6 PM Saturday night in Madrid when we got off the plane. I remember this because the guys that met me at the terminal were in uniform on a Saturday night and they were covered in grease. I thought, "What did I get myself into?"

I had no idea that this was just the tip of the iceberg. I was taken to a dormitory that looked like a battle zone; the dorm manager's name was Jesus: no kidding. As I walked into the manager's office I had to step over four of five people passed out on the floor. There was a piece of black slate in the middle of the room that was a pool table at one time, now it served as a cool place for an intoxicated GI to pass out, at least I didn't have to step over him. What was previously a television set was now a new place to stash the balls from the pool table, the tube was gone and the chassis held what was left of the balls from the table that weren't outside on the ground. Jesus gave me a key and told me how to get to my room.

I was led to a third floor room. When I opened the door I looked into a room that was void of any creature comforts except for a set of bunk beds. There was a wall closet and a desk and chair. It looked uninhabited. Not one item adorned the walls, it looked and felt like a jail cell; the place I would spend the next two years of my life. There was one very out-of-place item in the room; a telescope set next to the window pointed at the building next door. I felt overwhelmed. Was it the flight, was it the welcome at the terminal, or was it the stark and cold room that I stood in? I lay on the bed and cried, a 21 year-old sobbing like a baby, I never felt more alone. It was about to get worse as if that were possible!

I must have cried myself to sleep. I was a physical and mental wreck from a combination of the death of my grandmother, the trip from Michigan to the east coast then on to Spain, and the reality of being in a foreign country not knowing a soul and then walking through hell to get my room assignment. Then I met my roommate. It was now ten or eleven PM when a key slipped

A SPIRITUAL ROLLER COASTER

into the lock and the door swung open. In walked a disheveled young man in his early twenties. He proceeded to the desk where he removed an item, the size of a candy bar wrapped in foil, from his pocket. He them turned to me and asked if I wanted to smoke some Hashish with him!!!

ARE YOU KIDDING ME! I heard several horror stories before going to Europe about how the authorities in several countries dealt with drug use and possession: very severely. While I was in Turkey on a short tour of duty (TDY), I visited three Americans held in a Turkish prison for possession of drugs; it was not pleasant. I was terrified. I was sure that the security police would bust through the door at any time and I would be in jail for the rest of my life. I can't even remember if I prayed that night or not, but as tired as I was, sleep did not come that night. I knew I needed to get out of there as soon as possible. The next day I told the dorm manager I wanted a new room, how could it be worse. The guy in that first room was already on his way out of the service for drug abuse; I would find out later he was one of many.

Being a weekend it was a little difficult to find Jesus the dorm manager but I did and he assigned me to a new room. When I walked into the room it was apparent that someone lived there. The walls in this room seemed to be completely covered with a collage of posters, pictures, and other paraphernalia. The room was neat and clean but the occupant was not there. Based on a cursory glance I thought this was definitely a step up so I walked in and put my bag in the empty wall locker and went to grab a bite to eat at the chow hall. I also walked around the base to get acquainted with my new surroundings. I still didn't know anyone and it seemed that nobody was in a real hurry to make my acquaintance. I found out later that the Office of Special Investigation (OSI), the military version of the FBI, had people working covertly in the dormitories busting people for drug use and possession and black-marketing American merchandise on the Spanish economy. Any new person living in the dorm was suspect. Friends were hard to find but you didn't have to look far to find trouble.

I returned to the room late in the afternoon and there was still no sign of my roommate. It goes almost without saying in the military that when you go into a room that is already occupied you don't move anything until you ask the current occupants permission. Not knowing when he would return, I started looking around the room to get an idea about what we might have in common. I discovered, much to my chagrin, that it was probably very little.

The first items I noticed were two ceramic black skulls on a shelf, no big deal. I also noticed some knives and swords again no big deal, Spain was known for their quality swords and they made for unique decorations along with the wild colored posters and naked women adorning the walls. It wasn't until I got to the bookshelf that my blood ran cold... The titles of the books sent chills up my spine: "Demon Children" the Satanic Bible, and a book of Runes were just three of the many books dealing with Satanism and witchcraft. I was almost afraid to meet this guy now, especially considering what I'd already been a witness to so far.

The jet lag was now catching up with me. Even though it was still early in the evening, I was exhausted and wanted to go to bed. The thought of falling asleep in this room without knowing whom I was sharing the

A SPIRITUAL ROLLER COASTER

room with left me quite unsettled. It was obvious that this person slept on the bottom bunk so I jumped on the top bunk and fell into a restless sleep. Around midnight I awoke to the sound of the door opening. It was very dark in the room and I had no idea if he knew he was sharing his room until he walked in. He didn't turn on a light but lit a candle. At first I thought he was being considerate and thought maybe this guy isn't so bad after all. The candle cast an ominous shadow around the room allowing me to see the silhouette of a tall thin man.

He then did something I had never seen before. He put the candle in the middle of the floor, took the book of Runes from the shelf and sat on the floor with the book and candle in front of him. Sitting with his legs crossed and his hands resting on his knees, palms up, he opened the book, and began to chant as if reading from the book set in front of him. I didn't move. I was ignorant about what was happening in front of me, but I really didn't want to know either. The glow from the candle illuminated his face as he chanted; it was a ghostly white color.

There wasn't a sound in the room or the hall except for his voice and my heart pounding in my chest. As crazy as it sounds, I found myself thinking, "No wonder he doesn't have a roommate, he sacrifices them." He then picked up the book and candle and stood up. When he blew out the candle, I was almost paralyzed with fear. I had no idea who this person was or what he was capable of. I just knew everything I'd seen to this point made me wish I were anywhere but here. Again, sleep was not an option that night. The next day I went to see Jesus again. The irony is that the Jesus I should have been talking to was the furthest person from my mind.

I figured at this point that he was either playing a

cruel practical joke on the new guy or was not paying much attention to where he was putting me. Either way, I was hoping he was sick of seeing my face and would put a little more consideration into my next room assignment. As they saying goes, the third times a charm. My third roommate, in as many days, turned out to be a partying, womanizing, jock. He was the closest thing to normal I thought I'd get for a roommate. As it turns out, we would become very good friends.

He introduced me to his friends who were all pretty normal as far as I was concerned. I met some good folks at my shop and ended up traveling around Europe and having a great time while I was there but I fell further away from the Lord in the process. This led to me making several decisions that I probably wouldn't have made if my relationship with God were my priority at the time. I was concerned with one thing: making myself happy. God was trying to tell me at the very beginning of this journey that I needed to be talking to Jesus and it wasn't the dorm manager, but I didn't. And even though I left God out of the loop, He never left my side (Hebrews 13:5). and turned my mistakes into lessons that would eventually bring me back to Him. "And we know that in all things God works for the good of those who love him, who have been called according to his purpose" (Romans 8:28). I would add that He does this even when we are not seeking His will.

One decision I made that would change my life was to involve myself with a young married woman shortly before my departure from Spain and my separation from the Air Force. I knew it was wrong to involve myself with her but when she told me she was separated from her husband, I figured what's the harm. It didn't take us long to strike up a relationship even though I would be leaving in a few short months.

Home Alone...For Awhile

It came time for me to return to the states and I wondered if I would ever see her again. She was a new arrival when we met and had 18 months remaining on her tour when I left Spain. I figured I'd probably never see her again and it was probably for the best but I already cared deeply for her. We stayed in touch by mail. Overseas phone calls were extremely expensive in the early 1980's but we talked a few times by phone too. This went on for about three months and then she wrote and said she was getting out of the service and needed a place to stay. She wasn't close to her family and I was overjoyed that she wanted to stay with me. She eventually became my wife and the mother of my first two children.

I kept thinking this was the answer to prayers even though I had no relationship with God at the time, short of an occasional visit to church and a selfish prayer thrown up every once in a while when I wanted something to suit me. We struggled together as most young couples do, the situation made worse by the use of alcohol and an out-of-control temper. Neither of us had good parenting examples as far as relationships went but we continued to make a go of it. After struggling financially for two years, moving from job to job, I reenlisted in the Air Force and received an assignment to northern Michigan. We still struggled but things seemed to begin falling into place even though God was still not part of the picture, but it wasn't for His lack of trying.

2 BACK IN THE AIR FORCE AND CHURCH

Shortly after reenlisting and moving to Michigan from Ohio, we started attending church. We began to feel comfortable attending a local church and decided to get married. We asked the pastor of this church to marry us but he refused because of my fiancée's divorce and because we were living together. It took much coaxing to get her to go to church to begin with and we were trying to do what was right; but, when he refused to marry us, my wife and I would not set foot in a church again for several years.

Just when it looked as though we were getting on solid ground in our relationship with the Lord, and each other, we stumbled. We felt rejected by the very people we looked to for comfort and guidance. We tried to explain our situation and how we got there but to no avail. We married in our home shortly after leaving the church. That was my first real experience dealing with a judgmental person of the clergy and how it affects our witness.

It took the death of a friend to get us back into church and it wasn't to attend the funeral. His jealous wife shot him to death. It was a very difficult time for my wife and I especially in regard to our relationship. As we struggled to make sense of this senseless killing, I knew that the only way we would feel any peace was to ask God to help us. As we began to trust Him, things started happening; it was obvious that He was listening.

One event really stands out in my mind. Because we

were so close to our friend and his wife, we found ourselves in the middle of the investigation. As criminal investigations tend to go, this process was dragging on and on. I asked for a transfer to get away from what was going on, in a small town where everyone tends to know your business anyway, without a scandal, this was proving to be more than we could take. The transfer was granted; however we could not leave until the case closed. My wife was now pregnant and the emotional strain was really beginning to take its toll. We thought everything was set to go to trial and at the last minute there was another delay. When the prosecutor's office called me to tell me about the postponement, I couldn't believe it!

I hung up the phone and walked into the shop's tool crib where I could be alone. I prayed that God would put an end to this mess so we could leave that place and put this horrible episode in our life behind us. Our marriage was difficult before this happened; it's amazing that we stayed together. A fresh start in a new location with a baby on the way seemed to be exactly what we needed. All this was going through my mind as I prayed. Not even 30 minutes after saying that prayer, the phone rang and it was the prosecutor saying that he reached a plea bargain in the case; it was over.

We were attending church for about five months when the call came that the case closed. We were part of a young married couples group and both actively involved with planning and directing group events. We were growing in the Lord and our marriage was growing stronger too. It was as if God was giving us time to grow in these difficult circumstances before we moved on and left our church family behind. During this time, my wife accepted Christ as her Savior and followed in believer's baptism. We had been through many difficult trials and it seemed as if things were changing for the better.

Crawfish Anyone?

Moving to Louisiana was a culture shock for us. It seemed everything was different. The most noticeable thing to us was the social stratification. It was apparent in all facets of society: education, employment opportunities, social activities, housing, and especially religion. The little church we attended in Michigan, prior to moving to Louisiana, was devoid of the typical religious trappings common in many places of worship; this was very attractive to both of us. Our background, race/ethnicity, how we dressed, or what our current beliefs about particular vices might be didn't matter. The way this congregation looked at Christianity was... we're glad you're here to worship with us and they let God do the rest. This is not what we found when we moved.

We immediately began searching for a church home after relocating. One of the first places we visited turned out to be very disappointing. It was in a rural area so we had every reason to believe that it would be much the same as the church we left, although the building looked much bigger and much more modern than the one we left in Michigan; it was a very humble little church. If we could raise 120 dollars during an annual mission campaign, we were delighted. What we saw during our first visit to this new church was disturbing.

As we walked into the sanctuary, we quickly noticed a huge thermometer on the front wall. The number on top of the thermometer was 10,000 dollars. I remember thinking to myself how impressive it would be to raise that much money for mission support. I also noticed that everyone dressed to the hilt and there was nobody of a different race or culture in attendance. We were very conspicuous and felt very uncomfortable in our casual dress. We sat down and waited for the service to start. When the pastor walked in, he immediately focused our attention to the huge thermometer on the wall. I couldn't believe what I heard next.

The thermometer indicated that the church was about three-quarters of the way to their goal of 10,000 dollars. The preacher exclaimed that they were almost to their goal and the church could get their new tractor and sprinkler system! He them went on to single out people and talked about how much they did or didn't give. I couldn't believe it. We had already decided we weren't coming back and it took a tremendous amount of effort not to get up and walk out. This wasn't the end of our experience though. We signed the visitor's book on the way into the church; consequently a visitor came to our home from the church.

We lived in a tiny two-bedroom home, in a very modest part of town, close to the Air Force base. It was July in the Deep South and all we had was a little window air-conditioning unit to cool our home. My wife was now a very uncomfortable seven months pregnant and we just experienced our first southern monsoon... Our house was hot and partially flooded. We were trying to get a room ready for the baby's arrival and still trying to unpack and catalog our household goods recently delivered in a big pile in the back of a moving truck. We had cockroaches big enough to saddle and ride running around the house and we were a little homesick on top of everything else. It was in the midst of all this that the churches' choir director came to visit our home.

We knew we weren't going back to that church but we didn't want to be rude so we invited him in. I was painting in the baby's room when he arrived. I heard him introduce himself and where he was from and my wife offered him something to drink. After some small talk, I mentioned the thermometer and the preachers' reference to the giving practices of some of the congregates. He dismissed it as good-natured ribbing and tried to convince me of the relevance of collecting that money for the good of the church. I then mentioned the fact that, even though there was a large population of minorities in the area, there were none in the service when we visited their church; again, I couldn't believe what I heard. He said, "That's the way they like it and that's the way we like it." At that point there was no more discussion and we asked him to leave.

Our search for a church continued even after this rather unpleasant experience. We attended several different churches trying to find a place we felt comfortable but we couldn't seem to find that place. I was getting to know some of the people at work and one of my co-workers invited us to his church one Sunday. I accepted, and even though we didn't feel completely at home, we felt better there than the other places we visited. We continued going for a few weeks and began to feel a little better about attending there. My wife made the observation one Sunday after church that she was one of a very few number of women that wore slacks to church. I told her not to worry, God doesn't care how you're dressed as long as your heart's in the right place.

It wasn't but a couple weeks later, as we were leaving church, that the proverbial nail was put in the coffin. I felt more comfortable about this church than my wife did. Maybe it was because I was more willing to overlook certain issues, or that I worked with some of the people; but our presence there was tenuous to say the least. It would all be a mute point. As we left the church, a few of the women approached my wife. I thought maybe they were going to invite her to join them for some type of social function. To my total disbelief, one of them commented about what she was wearing. The woman suggested that, if we were going to attend church there on a regular basis, my wife should consider wearing dresses to church; I thought, are you kidding me?

Satan can manipulate us in very subtle ways. He knew it wouldn't take much for us, especially my wife, to throw in the towel and say who needs this. I tried to do some damage control. I asked the woman why she would suggest something like that. She replied that the Bible said so. I asked where I might find that verse of scripture and she referred me to a verse in the Old Testament, "A woman must not wear men's clothing, nor a man wear women's clothing, for the LORD your God detests anyone who does this" (Deuteronomy. 22:5). I mentioned that Jesus wore a garment similar to what our culture would consider a dress. We never went back... This was the last time my wife would go to church on a regular basis. I wouldn't return for several years.

Who Needs Church Anyway?

At this point, we didn't see much use in church. We carried on with our lives. The birth of our daughter brought a time of contentment and great joy in our lives. We still struggled with conflict but it didn't seem as unmanageable as before. My career was going well and I was going to school. My wife also had a good job and life seemed to be pretty good. Four and a half years after the birth of our daughter, our son was born. Shortly after that, I finished graduate school and began teaching at a local community college. I was proud of the fact that I was teaching college and I thought I had all the answers to life's most important questions. I thought I had everything figured out. I didn't. God had not been a priority in my life in many years. Knowing what I know now, He had never really been a priority.

The absence of God in our lives and marriage opened some huge holes in our relationship that Satan wasted no time in exploiting. Alcohol and anger were still issues. We never really learned effective conflict management or resolution skills and now differing personal interests and financial strains complicated the picture, but I still thought I had all the answers; I could fix everything. We managed to work through so many obstacles in the past to hold our marriage together; I had no reason to believe this time would be any different. But this turned out to be the beginning of the end...

I counseled many people for a variety of reasons over my career and I seemed to have a good track record of helping others but I always figured it was common sense that I shared with others and anyone could do what I was doing. I did think myself special because others felt they could confide in me and I did think I was good at helping others. It seemed I could help others solve their problems but the same wasn't true where my own life was concerned. In retrospect, I know that my pride was my biggest enemy.

By relying on my own foolish wisdom, I was usurping God's power in my life and destroying any possibility to save my marriage. My relationship with God was one of convenience at this point; I called on Him when I needed something but that was about it. It is hard to say what might have been, but I know that if my relationship with God were where it should have been, the events of the past and next several years would have been much different. The final outcome may have been the same, but the events leading up to that point would have been very different.

Without God's guidance, I made some very bad choices. My first bad choice was choosing not to fellowship with other Christians by attending church and not maintaining a relationship with Christ. This opened the door for Satan to grab the reins of my life and steer it down a path of regrets. The more I tried to handle problems on my own, the worse they became. My marriage was failing. My wife was spending a considerable amount of time away from home. This caused more anger on my part and it became a vicious circle. I tried finding peace in work, my children, and even Martial Arts. I was looking in all the wrong places. Family, work, and hobbies are all noble pursuits but what I was searching for was something only God can provide.

I tried everything "I" could think of to try to make my wife happy. I immersed myself in her primary interest: horses. I knew nothing about them and was very uncomfortable at first. The more I learned, the more I enjoyed them and the lifestyle that is part of owning horses. My daughter really enjoyed them too. This was added motivation to learn more about them. It seemed however, that no matter how hard I tried, it wasn't enough. She was still slipping away. We then bought a new house, maybe that would help having a place to call our own. I lived there a little more than a year.

3 IT'S OVER

We survived so many bad situations over the years but not this. I began keeping a journal in November of 1992. It chronicles the disintegration of our marriage and my frame of mind while it was happening. I blamed everyone else for what was happening. My focus was myself. Only after I rededicated my life to Christ was there a marked difference in my journal entries. But it took losing everything before I got down on my knees and asked God for forgiveness and help. He was more than happy to answer my prayers but not the way I imagined.

From the time we stopped attending church together until the time I found myself begging God's forgiveness, He tried on numerous occasions to get my attention, sometimes quietly and sometimes by dropping me on my head but I was too stubborn and proud to listen. It's amazing that God doesn't turn His back on us even when we completely ignore Him. Equally amazing is the fact that He still tries to communicate with us in subtle and not so subtle ways. So many times, He tried to get my attention. It started out very subtle but the more I dismissed Him the more obvious His messages became. But by now, I was so far away from Him, I didn't notice.

In November of 1994 I moved into a dorm room on the base where I was stationed. It broke my heart. The thought of not being with my children everyday and being away from my wife was extremely difficult. The combination of being emotionally hurt, lonely, frustrated, and most damaging, being away from the Lord, opened a gigantic door for Satan to waltz into and he did. Temptation comes in many forms but so do messages from God. The question is which will we focus our attention on? What and/or who do we chose to follow?

When I moved into the dorm and even prior to that, I began praying more and reading my Bible on occasion but I was still in a spiritual stupor. As I said before, God had been trying to get my attention but I kept ignoring Him. He was still trying when I moved into the dorm. I finished moving everything into the room and closed the door. On the back of the door was a little card someone had left stuck to the back of the door; it read, "With God, all things are possible." That is if you ask.

I continued to visit my wife and kids hoping that somehow this would all work out and we could put our family back together. My wife also had some decisions to make, both spiritually and personally, if we were to heal our family. Until that happened, there was no chance of resolution. One evening, after another very hurtful event, I made a phone call that changed the course of my life. Eventually it would be for the better, getting me back in touch with the Lord, but not initially. But, this is a great example of how something Satan intended to hurt and destroy, God used for good.

I called a woman that I'd spoken with on a few occasions. I told myself I just wanted some company. I went to her apartment and we had a real nice visit. She was very attentive and kind and it felt nice having someone fuss over me a little. I stayed for a few hours and we talked about many things including my marital situation. I told her I loved my wife very much and that I really wanted to keep my marriage together, talk about mixed messages. I gave her a hug and thanked her for a nice evening. I knew if I went back, it would be very difficult not to give into temptation. A few nights later I returned.

God never stopped trying to get me to listen even in the situation I now found myself in. I tried to justify my actions by telling myself that my wife was making absolutely no effort to keep our marriage together; but I knew I was wrong regardless of the circumstances. One evening, after having dinner at her apartment, she said she wanted to watch Charles Stanley on television. At the time, I had no idea who this guy was. I never had much use for preachers on television but this guy was different. As I sat and listened, it didn't take long to be overwhelmed with conviction. The topic of the message was adultery! I didn't listen to the subtle messages but I couldn't ignore this one if I wanted to. It hit me right between the eyes. It wasn't the first time I'd get clobbered over the head and, unfortunately, it wouldn't be the last.

I returned home, shortly after that, at my wife's invitation. She knew that I was seeing someone else; I had told her. I figured it really wouldn't matter much to her because she had what she wanted, but as I showed less interest in her she began to show more in me. I was happy that she was paying more attention to me but feeling very guilty at the same time. I knew there would be no peace in my heart or our relationship if I were not completely honest with my wife about my indiscretion. It did matter; I moved out again in March of 1995. This is when my life truly changed.

Lord, You have My Attention

I was on my way home from work to the little trailer I was now living in by myself. I was struggling with the events of the past couple years and contemplated how and why things turned out as they did. I had not eaten or slept, to speak of, in four days and was very depressed. I wondered how God could allow this to happen to me. As I approached a church, that I passed everyday on my way to and from work, something (the Holy Spirit) compelled me to turn into the church; it was the middle of March 1995 on a Wednesday night. A voice inside my head said that there is a young pastor here that can help. Several years before, while searching for a new church home after leaving Michigan, we visited this church one time and the pastor was an elderly gentleman so I had know idea who the pastor might be.

It was 6:15 PM when I walked into the church and I knew I probably wouldn't be able to talk to the preacher that night but maybe I could make an appointment for the next day. I asked a couple people if they knew where the pastor was and I found him a couple minutes later in the Sunday school building next to the church. He was young; I introduced myself and told him I'd like to make an appointment to speak with him. It was now 6:25 and Bible study was due to start in five minutes so I expected him to tell me to call in the morning for an appointment. I knew nothing about him at the time so what he did next surprised me.

I must have looked as bad as I felt that night because he excused himself and said he'd be right back. A couple minutes later, he returned and we retreated to an empty room and after a brief introduction and prayer we talked... for three hours! This man I had never laid eyes on, before this meeting, counseled with me for over three hours that night. What a servant's attitude! He found someone to teach the Bible study at the last minute so he could talk with me. That says nothing of the person that filled in at the last minute, but I found this attitude typical of the people of this church when I started attending there the next week.

After three hours of confession, tears, and prayer, I left the church, stopped to get a big chicken dinner at Church's Chicken (no kidding), and went home and slept like a baby. I'd like to say that I lived happily ever after but I still had to deal with the consequences of my actions. I experienced many emotional and spiritual ups and downs over the next few years but I never gave up on reconciliation with my wife in spite of overwhelming obstacles. I also continued to grow in my relationship with the Lord. A few significant events happened along the way that made no sense at the time, but in retrospect, seem crystal clear now.

I've always loved drama. I acted in plays in both high school and college so when the church decided to do the play "Heavens Gates, Hells Flames" I thought I'd audition. It was an incredible experience! Reality Outreach Ministries travels around the world producing and directing the play using the local congregants to play the parts. It's a whirlwind production. They arrive on Friday night and set up the stage. Auditions are Saturday morning, rehearsal Saturday night and Sunday afternoon, and the first performance is Sunday night! I played the part of Satan, a part I did not want.

I didn't wear a special mask or elaborate costume. They covered my face with black and white face paint and put red sparkles in my hair. This was going on while the whole cast was praying. We prayed for a whole hour each night before we took the stage. The production crew and cast hid my face from view until it was time for me to go on stage. The audio equipment made my voice sound low and guttural when I spoke into the microphone. During the production promotion, people were warned that the play might be too intense for children under eight but, when I walked out on stage and began talking and pointing at people in the crowd, adults got up and walked out.

A church that normally held two-to-three hundred people boasted a crowd of nearly a thousand for the two scheduled nights and the extra night the production crew stayed over due to the incredible response. Hundreds of people made decisions for Christ in those three nights! It was an absolutely unbelievable experience to be a part of. That was in the fall and Christmas was coming up fast. Our choir director always planned something very special during the holidays, and just a couple months after playing Satan, the choir director asked me if I wanted to play Jesus in the Christmas play: Wow! Talk about a contrast in character!

It was another awesome experience. I must say it was much easier playing Satan than it was playing Jesus. It was easy to be mean and nasty and let the hate flow from me because of what I was going through at the time but it was quite a different story playing Jesus. The most difficult part was when everyone gathered around me in a display of worship. I found it to be very uncomfortable and very humbling. Both of these experiences did a great deal to solidify my relationship with Christ. It was very uplifting to be a part of both these performances and see the tremendous response from those seeking Christ. But I was still dealing with the loss of my family. I still spent much time in God's Word and on my knees trying to understand why God was seemingly absent in helping me deal with my marriage. But at least now I was seeking the Lord's guidance and had a personal relationship with Jesus.

I continued a dialogue with my wife and I had my children any and all the time. There were lots of children in the park where I lived and we were always doing something when they came to visit. Many times, I felt that there was hope for reconciliation then the hammer would drop again. I remember asking my pastor, who by now was a good friend, how long was I to endure this painful emotional roller coaster. He asked me how long I was in it for, two weeks, two months, two years, or ten years? I told him whatever it took. He then said just trust God... I did.

In May of 1996, I moved home again. It really didn't feel right but I figured once I got back home, we could get things worked out. Again, I was doing it Tom's way not God's way. Three months later I moved back into the same place and even got the same phone number. Even though I knew I would probably never live at that house again, I remained faithful to my Lord and my wife. God was really working on me now, not that He wasn't trying before, but now I was paying attention and I was much more willing to yield to Him. I had a great church home and family and my kids went with me most Sundays. It was at this time that I met a young man that would eventually become one of my best friends.

Winning Others to Christ

I was working as a midshift supervisor and he was one of the crew chiefs on the shift. He was a nice enough guy but not one I would picture as a friend let alone a close friend. One night the subject of Christ came up at work and one of the guys on his crew started getting rude. He told him he could leave and didn't need to be part of the discussion if he was going to be so objectionable. He quieted down and eventually left, as did the rest of the people on the shift. We finished a little early so I let everyone go for the night. Everyone left but one. His interest about Christ compelled him to stay and talk more. I had no place to go, but an empty trailer, so we talked.

One thing was very obvious during our discussion; he had a very bad taste in his mouth about attending church. Like so many other people, he had some bad experiences with religious people. This was something that I was, unfortunately, too familiar with, but now much better equipped to deal with. (I will discuss this topic more in a subsequent chapter about religion.) As we talked, I explained that he could continue to use those bad experiences as an excuse not to go to church or realize that most of these folks understood that they weren't perfect and that's why they attended church, they know they need it, some just learn faster than others.

We talked for a couple hours and I asked him if he knew where he would go when he died; he said no. He seemed to want to take the step of faith to receive Christ but something was holding him back. He kept trying to find excuses not to ask Christ to be his savior and then said what so many others feel, God doesn't want me, I'm not good enough; I'd mess up the whole kingdom. I told him God did want him, nobody was good enough, and I already messed up the kingdom! I then prayed with him as he invited Jesus into his heart and life.

What a Change!

He was on fire for the Lord. He couldn't get enough of what the Bible said and I got calls at all hours of the night asking for help in understanding a verse of scripture. I really didn't mind the late night calls and felt good about helping someone else grow in the Lord. We were in the same Sunday school class and became close friends. He had a son a year younger than mine and we would get together on the weekends and do stuff with the boys. At the same time, three other very good friends of mine were dealing with separations and divorce too.

All of us were trying to hold together marriages that our wives no longer wanted to keep together and it wasn't because of the way they were treated by their husbands. Some nights we would sit together and try to provide support to one another but most nights we would watch a good movie and laugh about the days events. During this time my relationship with the Lord continued to strengthen and soon it was put to the test.

Enough is enough...

One night, my wife called and told me something that really upset me; it was now February of 1997. I was so upset about what she said, I determined, after I hung up the phone, that I was finished with this marriage; I couldn't take anymore. It was late and I went to bed. Usually, I would sleep on something, regardless of how upset I was, and would feel different about it in the morning; but I didn't sleep that night. I had already seen an attorney and had some preliminary paperwork drawn up shortly after I moved out the first time. I carried it in my briefcase for two years and figured this was it; it was time to end this marriage.

> I asked my pastor if he could recommend an attorney to me that would not inflame the situation. I told him I wanted a Christian attorney that valued the marriage covenant. I wanted someone that might be able to help me hold my marriage together and if that wasn't possible, keep it from becoming an ugly scenario that would cause a huge riff between us and hurt the kids even more than they already were. He gave me his recommendation and I set up an appointment to meet with him. This fellow was great! He

sent a very personal letter to my wife stating that I visited him and I did not want to divorce but could not continue in this marriage as it was. He recommended we go to a counselor together and he would refrain from filing the papers in court. She agreed to the counseling but quit after just a couple visits.

After not sleeping all night, I was sure about my decision. I was working second shift and figured I would stop by the little boutique she opened and pay her the courtesy of letting her know I was filing for divorce and to expect the paperwork. I was dressed and ready to walk out the door when I opened my briefcase and pulled out the divorce papers to look at them. When I opened the correspondence, the first paragraph I looked at said something about separation and having not reconciled. I immediately thought to myself, "I know what this says, why am I looking at it again?" It was depressing enough without reading over it again. I folded it up and put it back in my briefcase.

I was about to walk out the door when I realized I didn't do my devotion so I sat down and opened to the devotion for that day, the day before my sons sixth birthday. The title was "Be Reconciled, Let God Heal Your Relationships" Are you kidding me? I thought God had a warped sense of humor at this point but there was no ignoring the message. I proceeded to her boutique and told her of my intentions. I also told her the only reason I wasn't going to see my attorney was because I wasn't going to disobey God again. She obviously didn't sleep the night before either.

4 FATHER REALLY DOES KNOW BEST

This is a perfect example of God knowing the big picture while we only see our present circumstances. About one month after I decided to heed what I was sure to be a message that God didn't want me to file for divorce, I received orders to Kunsan Air Base, Korea. This was a remote assignment, which meant I couldn't take my family with me. Again, I found myself wondering why God would want me on the other side of the world when my family life was in complete chaos. It was clear now why the divorce should be put on hold but how could this help my marriage relationship. It wasn't that relationship God was working on but I couldn't see that at the time.

I tried everything to get out of my assignment. My commander, First Sergeant, supervisor, attorney, pastor, and even my wife submitted letters, to the proper authorities responsible for assignments, on my behalf explaining why this assignment should be canceled. It was a one-year assignment and I was 18 months from retirement. But after every possible appeal, I was shipped to Korea July 4th 1997.

A Time in the Desert

This was definitely a time of testing for me, my proverbial desert, you might say. This place can make or break a person in many ways but especially spiritually. Every kind of temptation known to man is available in abundance. Alcohol and women of any flavor were available on and off base. Being on the other side of the world adds to the temptation because distance and loneliness make it is very easy for a person to rationalize poor behavior. They say to themselves, "who will ever know" or "I need to make myself feel better."

Fortunately, there was an equally formidable ministry program available, staffed with very loyal, dedicated, knowledgeable, and most importantly, compassionate servants of Christ. The chapel offered several services in many different venues. The two I found most inspiring were the protestant and gospel services. Because resources, including manning, can be hard to acquire at a remote location, the chapel staff could not offer a service designed for every different protestant denomination. All protestant denominations attended one service and it was awesome!

Some theologians frown on the concept of ecumenical worship. They point to passages in the Bible that speak of the ecumenical movement of the False Prophet and the Antichrist. In his book "Revelation Unveiled" Tim LaHaye calls ecumenical church unity a plan of the devil and references Revelation 17:15 as the basis of this conclusion. In this context, I completely agree with his conclusion; however, I personally feel that each denomination serves different people and makes up a unique part of the body of Christ: the church. "Now the body is not made up of one part but of many" (1 Corinthians 12:14). And by understanding how each part functions in the body of Christ, we learn to appreciate instead of criticize each other. I also feel it is important to learn how to appreciate and respect those differences while maintaining Christian unity and purpose. The ecumenical service was a great way to do that.

By worshipping with people from different denominations, I experienced other ways to express my faith and love for Christ. I also learned a great deal about what others believe. I'm not talking about extreme, unbiblical beliefs mind you; I'm talking about learning why some believe in speaking in tongues, or that salvation can be lost, not if God is male or female or if homosexuality is right or wrong according to the Bible. This gave me a better understanding of my own faith and insight into the motives of others beliefs.

One of the most vital lessons learned from this experience is how much man incorporates religion into Christianity. Christianity is not a religion! Christianity means to be Christ-like, to be imitators of Christ. Jesus was not Baptist, Methodist, Lutheran, Catholic, or any other denomination. I'm sure He does not approve of some of the mandates different denominations incorporate into their doctrine in the name of the Bible, those man-made rules espoused by different faiths that scripture doesn't support. All these mandates do is turn people away from Christ instead of leading them to him.

Many lay people were also very active in the various ministries available to us while we were there. They brought many diverse talents to the different ministries. Some were incredible musicians, others talented speakers and teachers, some brought excellent counseling skills, while others were skilled organizers, some were great cooks, and some were computer experts linking us to loved ones in the states. All displayed a servant's attitude and contributed a great deal of time and talent to help make our stay a little more bearable. This included everyone active in the chapel community including our wing commander (The Wolf). The 8th Fighter Wing is called the Wolf Pack.

He was the most influential person on base, not because of his position but because of his compassion for others.

This man practiced what he preached and his support for the chapel community was second to none. Every Friday night a different squadron on the base hosted a home cooked dinner at the chapel annex (named the Sonlight Inn) and on many occasions the Wolf was there asking about our families, our jobs, and helping us cook, serve, and clean up after the meal. I honestly don't think there was a person on the base that didn't like him. We were all a big family and he was the patriarch.

Another amazing way God used people to touch my life while I was in Korea was to introduce me to a cousin I had never met. A couple months before I left for Korea, I found out that a cousin, by marriage, received an assignment to the Korean Peninsula for the same period I would be there. He was about 100 miles north of my location, close to Seoul. We didn't even know what the other looked like so we had to tell each other what we were wearing to recognize each other the day we arranged to meet.

It was amazing how we both felt that we'd known each other for years even though we'd only spoke to each other over the phone, very briefly, on two different occasions. Although we were 100 miles apart, we visited each other once every couple of months. His faith in God was an added blessing. We always had a great time when we were together and we were even able to come back to the states on the same flight. It was just one more way God made my time in the desert a little easier to bare.

The time I spent in Korea was definitely the most challenging, rewarding, and satisfying of my military career both personally and professionally, and during that time, I learned what serving God and others is all about. I had the privilege of teaching the gospel to a small group of Korean nationals, working as a lay minister during worship services, singing in a praise band, counseling with people trying to deal with family separation, staffing support programs, being part of a Promise Keepers group, participating in a retreat with the American missionary to Kunsan, and visiting the largest Christian church in the world located in Seoul South Korea. God worked in me and through me in ways I never knew possible until then. I learned what faith was all about. As I said before, I could have easily gone in the other direction, but by the grace of God, I didn't.

The friendships I established during that time are not only the kind that last a lifetime, they are the kind that last an eternity. There were many very difficult times to endure but the good times far outweighed the bad. When it came time to return home, I found it very difficult to say goodbye to my extended family at Kunsan but it was time to move on. My time in the desert had come to an end. I tried everything humanly possible to get out of that assignment and could see absolutely no reason why God would choose that particular time in my life for me to leave my family. Thank God he did. I could only see my immediate circumstances; He could see the big picture. The pruning process started a couple years before but He was still grooming me for something. What, I wasn't sure of, but when the time is right, I'm sure I'll have no doubt.

Going Home...

I returned home July 3rd 1998. I hoped that, somehow, the separation and time away from my wife would help mend our marriage and family. I thought that my time away from her was more for her benefit, not mine. Again, I was wrong. Although we both had much to work through emotionally, I thought my time away was going to help her realize what life would be like without me in her life; I guess, in a way, it did. Right after my return to the states, I took the kids and went on a three-week vacation to Michigan to visit my family. It was great being home with my kids.

I really wanted to save my marriage but when both people don't share the same commitment to do so failure is inevitable. After returning from vacation, I lived at home for two very tense months. I tried to convince myself that everything would be fine after a period of adjustment but it wasn't to be. I moved out for the last time in October of 1998. I remember praying at the time that God would forgive me because I determined that if I moved out again, I would file for divorce.

It had now been nearly eight years since the beginning of the end of our marriage. God continued to work in my life and I had my children whenever I wanted them, and it was a blessing to have them all the time. Their mom never tried to use them as a weapon or leverage like many estranged spouses. She always made sure I got to spend as much time as I wanted with them. As I struggled to know if I was doing the right thing many events took place that encouraged me. First of all, I found a nice and affordable place to live. It was right between the base and the house where my children lived. My church was between the base and my home. My wife agreed to use my attorney too, this kept matters as simple and peaceful as possible under the circumstances.

As I said earlier, I asked my pastor to recommend a Christian attorney that valued marriage and would do everything in his power to keep us together: he did as much as he could and he'll probably never know how much he did to help us maintain a cordial relationship, benefiting our children tremendously. He sent her the letter mentioned previously, in an attempt to head off any legal action. He then agreed to allow us to both counsel with him about our legal matters; we'd already agreed on most issues. Then, on one occasion, while we were finalizing everything, he saw another opportunity to intervene and possibly save our marriage.

Is This Really Necessary?

The day before one of the meetings we had with our attorney, our son had a baseball game. There's usually a lot to talk and laugh about after watching seven and eight-year-olds play baseball. As our attorney was putting the finishing touches on the property and custody settlement, my wife and I discussed our son's game the day before. We laughed about a particular play he made and continued talking about the rest of the game. I'm sure our attorney thought it a bit strange that we could sit and laugh together in the midst of such proceedings. When I looked back at him, he was looking at us over the top of his glasses like a father ready to ask a question he knew would be very difficult to answer.

My wife and I were now looking at him and were no longer laughing. He looked at her and asked, "Do we really need to do this?" Her eyes filled with tears and there was a deafening silence in the room. I looked at her wondering how she might answer, was an eleventh hour reconciliation possible? After a brief pause, she simply said yes... He then looked back down and proceeded with what he was doing. My wife was quietly crying so I reached over and softly touched her hand and said everything would be okay. As I held her hand, my attorney looked up again and rocked back in his chair. What he said next, made me feel as if God was telling me that I was doing the right thing at the right time.

He said that in over 30 years of practicing law, he never

had a couple sitting in his office, talking about property settlements and child custody, holding hands and comforting each other. That was quite a statement but he continued, "thank you Jesus for letting me see this before I die." Wow! He then rocked forward, finished the paperwork, and showed us to the door. He called a couple days later to tell us that the date was set for our divorce; it was two days before our sixteenth wedding anniversary.

My wife and I went to the courthouse together. A long-time friend of ours agreed to be a witness for us. If I remember correctly, we were the first case. We all took the stand, answered a few questions from the judge, and in a matter of a few minutes, it was finished. We were together for over 18 years. It seemed very strange as we walked from the courthouse to think we were no longer married. I can't remember if I took her to her clothing boutique or if I took her home; I do remember giving her a kiss and hug and wishing her well.

Does God Understand?

Looking back, I feel that the course of events, after much pray about my decision to divorce, was an indication to me, that although I was doing something God hates (Malachi 2:16), He understood, if not blessed, my choice. Through the entire process, I grew closer to the Lord. It was only a couple months before my divorce that another event would change the course of my life. I flew to Michigan to interview for a job as I was nearing retirement from the Air Force and I attended my grandpa's 88th surprise birthday party at the church I grew up attending.

Events were happening incredibly fast in my life in the early part of 1999. In March, I flew to Michigan to interview for a position that I found on the Internet. I thought that if

I got the job and moved back to Michigan, it might afford my, now, ex-wife and I an opportunity to start over. I knew that it was in God's hands and I also knew that if she didn't move, I'd be a long way from my two great kids. But, I said, Lord it's in your hands. I missed Michigan and being close to family so it was a real treat to have the opportunity to be part of the birthday party my mom arranged for my grandpa.

When I was a kid, the church was always full on Sunday morning. There was always something going on. We had a basketball program, softball and bowling team, and lots of youth activities. It saddened me to look around the church the morning of grandpa's party and see a very small group in attendance and most of them were elderly. I remember thinking to myself what a joy it would be to pastor the church I grew up in and how awesome it would be to see it thriving again. At the time, it was a passing thought that seemed almost absurd. I got back on a plane and headed back to Louisiana.

Everyday, I walked to the mailbox wondering if today would be the day I would receive a reply about the job I interviewed for. I could hardly breath when I found it in the mail. I remember praying before I opened it telling the Lord that no matter the outcome, I trusted it was the right thing for me. To my delight, I received a generous offer and I was to start three weeks after starting terminal leave. I also had a line on a house that was exactly what I was looking for and my divorce would be final nine days before my scheduled departure. With everything going so well, I was sure God was greasing the way for me.

There was much going on in the world at the time and Iraq was a major concern again. Because there was so much uncertainty, the Air Force instituted the "Stop Loss" program. That meant nobody could separate or retire from the Air Force. It started a few days after I left the base but I was already on terminal leave. That meant I was using up my accrued leave. I was technically not retired until July 31st and it was only the end of May. I thought for sure I was going to receive a call telling me to return to my unit. I found out later that the only reason I wasn't called back was because I had already cleared the base and left the state. Others that stayed in the local area weren't as fortunate.

Everything seemed to be falling into place for me. I got the job and was moving home, I had a house in a perfect location that was exactly what I was looking for, and I didn't have to return to the military because of "Stop Loss." I was also going to have the kids for the summer so I had to hustle to get their rooms together before they got there, but I had no furniture. I lived in a small trailer in Louisiana and didn't have much furniture to speak of; I surely didn't have enough to furnish a 1,500 square-foot house. God took care of that too.

Once the word got out about my needs, I was overwhelmed with the generosity of family and friends. When I moved into my trailer the same thing happened. God used family, friends, and in some cases, people I hardly knew to provide me with exactly what I needed when I needed it. Before I knew it, I had more furniture and other household goods than I could use. What people didn't want back, I gave to charity. My kids couldn't believe it when they got here and they had their rooms all set up including wall hangings in the décor they each desired, his was sports, hers was horses. It was awesome!

How could there be any doubt that God was looking after my every need. Everything was Swweeeeeet! But as it does so often, prosperity leads to complacency, as it did in my case. I had a good paying job, a nice place to live, and my kids were with me, if only for the summer. I also had a couple weeks off before I started the new job to spend with my kids. I was still going to church, tithing, and doing my daily devotions but nothing more.

I Still Didn't Get It!

My thoughts were more about finding a girlfriend and how important I "thought" I was in my new job and not about how to serve the Lord. My relationship with the Lord was going in the wrong direction. As I focused more on worldly possessions and personal satisfaction, I became less aware of the Lord's prompting. You'd think by this time I'd know better. I was tired of God getting my attention by drastic measures but when things are going good, it is easy to forget the lessons learned.

God tried to get my attention in subtle ways, but again, I wasn't listening. I remember thinking, as I read through the Bible on several occasions, how crazy it was that the Israelites were hammered over and over again for straying from the Lord but they continued doing it miracle after miracle. I guess it's easier to do than you might think; at least it was for me.

Why is it that when our life seems to be cruising along that we forget about God when He's the one providing the smooth ride? Instead of thinking about how grateful we should be because of all the blessings in our life we start to think our good fortune is of our own doing. As we focus less on God and more on ourselves, we slowly begin to ease back into our old attitudes, habits, and actions. Maybe it's not so hard to understand the Israelites actions after all... I was about to learn another very painful lesson.

I thought my new job was going well and I was starting to get to know some of my coworkers. Training was also going well and I even started working on a database to streamline the process I was learning. I also felt I had a pretty good rapport with my supervisors and I was meeting people from other sections and learning more about the overall operation of the company. I enjoyed my work and the people I worked with. Then one day, right before I was ready to leave for the day, one of the people that interviewed me for the job said he needed to talk to me. I thought it strange that we went into an empty office and closed the door; I was completely unaware of what he wanted to talk about.

He seemed a bit uncomfortable and I was starting to wonder what the heck was going on. He then began by telling me there were complaints about things I said to different people; I had absolutely no idea what he was talking about. I listened in disbelief as he told me of discussions I had with people that were taken completely out of context. When asked about what was said by a representative of the personnel department, I denied nothing and told him this was wrong. I could sit here and point fingers all day long about the events that took place that led to this discussion, but that isn't important. What does matter is that, even though I confronted my accusers and felt vindicated after doing so, I lost my job anyway after only six weeks. What was I going to do now? How was I going to pay for my house? What was I going to tell my children? Why did this happen? I didn't do anything wrong? Why me Lord?

I picked up my kids and told them what happened. I only had a couple weeks left with them before they had to return to Louisiana for school so we just went on with our plans. I figured I could worry about everything after they were gone. In the meantime, I tried to be as upbeat as possible and prayed constantly. The funny thing about prayer is how your eyes open up to unseen things when you are paying attention. The paradox is that we generally don't pray from the heart until we are dealing with a difficult situation and that is when we seem to be more spiritually sensitive to what God is trying to tell us. Why can't we pay attention when things are going great? It didn't take long to find out the answer to the question, why me? Let's call it a lesson in focus.

As I said before, I thought I was important. I was just going through the motions of my faith and, consequently, I was slowing falling away from God. I remember, on many occasions, praying that the Lord would always keep me close to Him, and that I didn't want to live without Him in my life to help me with everyday decisions. It's cliché but true; be careful what you pray for. Even before I lost my job, I knew in my heart, I was losing my focus on the Lord, but I wasn't really concerned about it: He was!

So many times in the past, He tried to gently remind me of the direction I should be going and I didn't listen until I got the tire-iron over the head. This time was no different. He tried several times to redirect me before I got the tire-iron again. I prayed that He would keep me close to Him and He was. I must say that even though I still needed getting clobbered to wake up, it was now only once instead of several times.

I Think I Understand

As soon as I started paying more attention to my service to the Lord and less on myself, life got much better in a hurry. I was soon working as a college instructor with a great group of people and I was a substitute teacher in the local schools. It was a little strange working and getting paid on an "on call" basis but this kept me focused and required me to trust that God would provide for my needs.

As I learned to trust the Lord more, His purpose for my life was becoming clearer. Proverbs 3:5-6, "Trust in the LORD with all your heart and lean not on your own understanding; in all your ways acknowledge him, and he will make your paths straight." began to take on a whole new meaning for me.

The more I trusted the Lord, the easier it was for me to see the path in front of me. Someone once told me that Jesus lights our way for sure, but sometimes He only shows us a small portion of the road ahead until we are ready to see more. I know now what he was talking about. We must learn to trust Him to lead us down the path of life and if that means only lighting our way so we can only see a couple steps ahead of us until we learn to trust, that's what He does. The less we know and see, the more likely we are to hold on to his hand and follow Him. He wants us to let go of His hand without getting lost; as we grow in our faith, He let's go. It's a matter of trust.

The Bible says the Lord will never give us more than we can handle. "No temptation has seized you except what is common to man. And God is faithful; he will not let you be tempted beyond what you can bear. But when you are tempted, he will also provide a way out so that you can stand up under it" (1 Corinthians 10:13). He teaches us to handle more by providing for us when we trust Him. The more we trust, the more He provides and the more we trust. This is particularly true of our finances.

God knows that most of us can be very good about giving our time and service but are much more reluctant when it comes to our money. I had a real problem with this myself. That's why God challenges us to test Him on this point (Malachi 3:10). As far as I know, it's the only time in the Bible that He challenges us to test Him. But here He

I'd Like You To Meet Someone

proves His faithfulness too if we trust Him to provide for our needs. I'll speak more on this later.

One thing that is very important to note here is that even though I was out of work for about two months, I had what I needed to get by. The work and money I needed to pay my bills was there when I needed it. A couple of months later I met a woman who would later become my wife. I'm sure our meeting was no accident. I'm also sure that our meeting was a result of trusting the Lord. Neither of us was really looking for a companion when we met; but a person can never have too many friends, so we started out as friends. As it turns out, we were perfect for each other.

She was attending church when we met but she did not have a personal relationship with Jesus. I had the privilege of praying with her to accept Christ. One thing I was sure of was that I would not get involved with a woman that did not know Christ as her personal Savior and practice her faith. Our friendship continued to grow, as did our relationship with Christ. Fifteen months after we met we married and a little less that two years after that God blessed us with a beautiful baby girl; she was really a miracle baby and she's brought so much joy to so many already. At the time of this writing, she is seven months old.

My service to the Lord is now the purpose of my life. I know that when I make God my first priority, He takes care of everything else. I serve the Lord in many different capacities now. But what I want to do most is be like Christ and try to live my life to that end. I know I'll stumble and fall from time to time, but I hope that the light on the path minimizes the number of ruts I may come across. Recently, a good friend of mine called me and paid me the greatest compliment I could ever receive on earth. He told me he accepted Christ as his personal Lord and Savior due, in no small part, to how I lived my life trusting in the Lord to provide for my needs and because of my service to others.

I want to be that kind of an example for everyone around me. I don't hold myself to unrealistic standards of conduct or try to impress others in any way. I just try to do the best I can and trust the Lord with all my heart. I'll let God worry about the small stuff and it's all small stuff. My prayer is that I can be a little more like Jesus today than I was yesterday.

My life has been a spiritual roller coaster. I must admit that the times of sorrow were usually of my own accord. The lessons during this wild ride are plenty and valuable. The most important lesson I've learned is that everything I need to know about living my life, and dealing with the difficulties I face during my life, can be found written in God's word. I've also learned, by receiving counseling, being a student and teacher of psychology for many years, being the father of a child with a learning disability, and from counseling others, that secular counseling without a biblical foundation is futile.

Who Has The Answers?

People go to counselors for years without making progress because they are lead to believe that their confused emotional state and poor behavior are someone else's fault. Rationalization instead of confrontation is the order of the day. As long as people are not held accountable for their actions, they will not move forward. Authors of psychology textbooks convey the same sentiment unwittingly when they write that many times there are no explanations for psychological/emotional disorders and that once psychologists identify a new disorder and bring it to the public's attention, the number of people diagnosed with the newly identified disorder increases dramatically. Why is this?

Is it because there are really that many people that are ill that have never been identified or is it because we now have another excuse to act in ever-increasing selfish ways? Why is it that people involved with drugs, legal or illegal seem to have a much easier time winning their battles when Christ is the center of their life sometimes after years of struggling to beat their addictions on their own? Because, "With God, all things are possible" (Matthew 19:26).

That's what this book is all about... answers and where to find them. People may search their whole life for answers, for purpose, for meaning of life and come to one dead end after another. Why? Because they leave out the most important ingredient: Jesus! Sigmund Freud is a perfect example of this futility. Considered one of the great thinkers of all time, his arrogance and pride about his intellect and wisdom blinded him from what he saw as obvious... the presence of God.

Freud had a very low opinion of mankind and, based on everything I read about him, he was a very unhappy man for most of his life. He thought himself to be brilliant and reasoned anyone with common sense could not possibly believe in God. His conflicted views about religion added to his distress. Armand Nicholi illustrates this point very well in his book, *The Question of God*. He writes quoting Freud, "the religions of mankind must be classed among the mass delusions," and he referred to religion as "the universal obsessional neurosis of humanity." He wondered if "Jesus Christ is part of mythology" or merely "an ordinary deluded creature." Freud referred to the teachings of Jesus as "psychologically impossible and useless for our lives" and concluded,

"I attach no value to the 'imitation of Christ.'"

Later in the book Nicholi speaks of Freud's assertion that "God allows horrors" to occur and that he (Freud) will hold God responsible. Freud expresses his anger and defiance: "I...have no dread at all of the Almighty. If we were to meet I should have more reproaches to make to Him than He could to me." Nicholi finishes the thought with this very poignant statement, "Those who have suffered much perhaps can understand Freud's anger. But as an atheist, with whom is he angry?"[1]

Though many people considered Freud a genius, including him, he thought it foolishness to believe in an omnipotent, omnipresent God. But arrogance is blinding and the Bible tells us that the wisdom of man is foolishness to the Lord. "For the foolishness of God is wiser than man's wisdom" (1 Corinthians 1:25). Freud's arrogance led to a life of futility and emptiness. In the end, he took his own life.

We all feel an emptiness that we try to satisfy with all the world has to offer but to no avail. That void is one that can only be satisfied by the presence of Christ in our heart and life, by having a personal relationship with the creator and sustainer of all of us. One day we will all stand before our creator and give an account of our lives on earth. It is written: "As surely as I live, says the Lord, every knee will bow before me; every tongue will confess to God" (Romans 14:11). He will hold us accountable then; we should hold each other accountable now.

I share my story as a basis for what follows; concerns I have about the misconceptions about being a Christian and what the Bible says, and doesn't say, about a personal relationship with Christ. These concerns are based on my own spiritual struggle and the lessons learned along the way. I have never seen religion win a person to Christ; however, I've seen many people come to know Jesus because of those who truly strive to be imitators of Christ. I surly don't have all the answers but God does. Please open your heart as you continue to read, that He may speak to you even if you already know Him as your Savior.

CHOICES

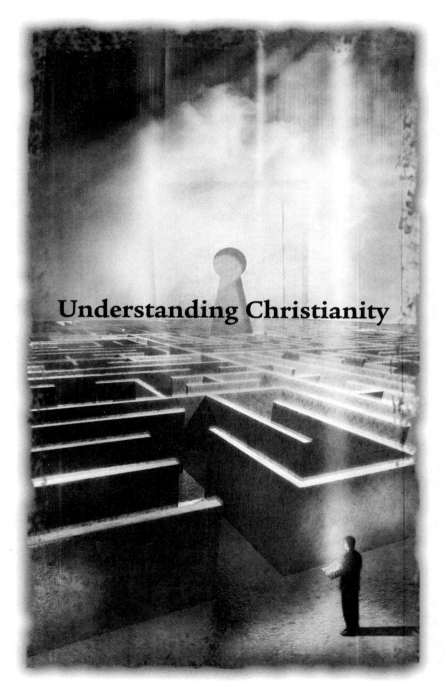

5 WHAT IS A CHRISTIAN?

What does it mean to be a Christian? I mentioned earlier that I accepted Jesus as my savior when I was 12 years old and was baptized on 28 February 1971. I believe that I knew exactly what I was doing and meant what I said when I prayed for forgiveness. Was I a Christian... in a word, yes, in practice, I had more to learn than I could ever imagine. I had no idea about the journey I just spoke of that would lead me to where I am today. I've always held to the belief that once you accept Christ you cannot loose the gift of grace and mercy received from the Lord through Christ. I believe this more than ever now... I'm a good example of why this is true, not to mention, I don't believe that God is in the business of giving away gifts only to take them back. I imagine He wouldn't approve if we gave something away only to take it back, why should we think He would do that?

I'd like to pose a few questions and views I have about being a Christian and what I feel I've learned during this 30 plus year journey. Who, what, and where is God. What does He expect of us in terms of how we should live our lives and treat others? How does he speak to us and get our attention? Why do we suffer? And why do bad things happen to good people.

I think one thing that humans are real good at is making things more complicated than they need to be... this includes Christianity. As I said before, I'm no expert on anything, especially the Bible and biblical history so I don't pretend to have any answers; these are just my observations and personal experiences over the last 30 years.

Like many young Christians, I was fired up about being a Christian at first but because I didn't stay in fellowship with God by reading the Bible and praying, it didn't take long for me to fall away from Him. I quit attending church too. I know, you don't have to go to church to believe in God or be a Christian but you should want to go so you can spend time with other Christians learning as much as you can about God's Word. I used all the excuses not to go to church: they twist the Bible around to say what they want it to say, all they want is my money, they're all hypocrites, and so on.

First of all

If you can read, you can see what the Bible says for yourself. Sometimes it takes a couple different translations and some research into ancient cultures to completely understand the context and message that a passage is trying to convey and sometimes that's not enough. Sometimes you have to pray for understanding and when all that doesn't seem to be enough, you just have to have faith. "Now faith is being sure of what we hope for and certain of what we do not see" (Hebrews 11:1). Why is it that we can believe some things in the Bible but not all of it? I've learned it doesn't work that way; it's an all or nothing proposition. The Bible says, "All Scripture is God-breathed and is useful for teaching, rebuking, correcting and training in righteousness" (2 Timothy. 3:16). I understand that to mean that God inspired man to record and compile everything in it, exactly the way He wanted it. It is the primary way He speaks to us.

I have read the Bible through from beginning to end in two different versions and I found many things that I didn't know were in there, many things that I had heard but were taken out of context, things that were common knowledge even if you don't go to church, but most interesting were the sayings I didn't find that many people said were in the Bible. A couple examples come to mind; first, the way we must dress for church.

In more than one church and denomination women must wear dresses and men must wear suits, especially if in a leadership position. I've heard people teach that the use of alcohol is forbidden and that the use of musical instruments in church and dancing is wrong. One of the most quoted fictitious bible verse is, "God helps those who help themselves." When, in fact, that is completely contrary to biblical teachings. What I found by reading the Bible is that all of these teachings are not biblically sound. There are other less obvious examples that require more study and guidance from the Holy Spirit. The Bible also makes it clear that until we accept Christ, God's word sounds like foolishness to us, "The man without the Spirit does not accept the things that come from the Spirit of God, for they are foolishness to him, and he cannot understand them, because they are spiritually discerned" (1 Corinthians 2:14). Once we accept Christ, His Spirit living inside us helps us understand His word!

As for praying

I figured what's the point, God knows what I need and how can He keep up with all the requests any way? Not to mention the likelihood of Him hearing my pray was probably next to none. Another tremendous mistake... I now know that God speaks to us through His word, among other things, but we speak to Him when we pray and He does hear us. I have had countless numbers of prayers answered. Some prayers were answered the way I'd hoped and others were not, but they were answered none the less. Reflecting on the prayers that were not answered, I realize that God's way was always much better than mine, I just couldn't see it at the time. I've heard it said that man has a point of view but God has the whole picture. How true.

When we read God's word He speaks to us, when we pray we speak to Him. When we don't fellowship with other Christians we tend to do neither and slowly start slipping away from Him. He always stays where He is; we are the ones that move away. But what's amazing about God is that He doesn't give up. We can hear His voice as we move away, but there comes a point that we've moved so far that WE don't hear Him anymore. He's still calling though; He never gives up.

Now let's talk about money.

I know, another favorite subject. It seems that when it comes to giving to God we are pretty good at giving our time, service, worship, and praise but when it comes to money we fall way short of the mark. I heard the words tithe and offering for years as I slipped in and out of different churches but I never did stop to think that the churches very existence depends on the gifts of those attending. I know there are many churches where a person wonders when enough is enough in terms of new buildings, technology, and staff. But that is between the pastor and members of that church and God. I've come to realize that when I find myself in a situation where I'm asking questions about how a church is using the gifts of the people, I must pray about it. If I'm uncomfortable, I can speak to the pastor and if I'm still not at ease I can always leave.

God makes it very clear in His word that we are to

support the church and other ministries with our tithes and offerings. In fact, in Malachi 3:8-10, He says when we don't tithe we are ROBBING Him! He takes it one step further than that; He goes on to say, "test me on this." It's the only place in the Bible, to my knowledge, where we find God challenging us to test Him. Maybe because He knows how tight fisted we can be. I know I was. I was forgetting that everything I have is from Him to begin with and I am only demonstrating my faith and obeying His word when I give back what is already His.

For years I heard people testify that they just started tithing and they always had enough to pay their bills. I'm thinking no way... you just don't take one-tenth of your income away and not miss it! But that robbing from God thing was really bothering me and every time I dropped a couple bucks in the offering plate, or even a five spot when I was feeling generous, I just didn't feel right. So I figured, why not give it a try? I've always been pretty careful about spending money, but it always seemed that I just had enough to get by, so I just couldn't imagine being able to tithe, but God says, "test me on this" so I did.

The next time I paid my bills, I took a tithe right off the top and completed writing out my bills... I had enough and then some! So I did it the next time and continue to this day. When things get tight, it is always tempting to blow off my tithe but I don't. And even though I make less now than I have in several years, I always have enough and have even been able to save a little bit without changing my quality of living. Don't ask me how, because I have absolutely no explanation except for God's faithfulness.

I have seen, first hand, how giving blesses many people in several ways. I received a tremendous blessing while in Kunsan Korea while serving in the Air Force in 1997-98.

An American missionary, Bill Stewart and his wife, ran a small mission in Kunsan City. Anyone was welcomed and many American servicemen and women found a few of the comforts of home there. This was not only a mission but it was also Bill's home where he raised his family. While we were there, he made it our home too. His presence in Korea was made possible primarily by the support of church family's from the states.

I have also seen storefront missions in action. These are places that those in need can receive foodstuffs, clothes, and other necessities. Again, made possible by the generosity of others. Some churches also have food and clothes pantries for those in need. I received food from one of those pantries for a time shortly after being assigned to a base in Michigan. Their gifts helped my new wife and I through some tough financial times. We may never see what a blessing our gifts may bring to someone, but God knows.

One last thought on this before I move on. Thinking that our gift won't be used for what it's intended can't restrict us. If we belabored this point, we would never give. There's nothing wrong with checking the reputations of churches and other charitable organizations, but again, it boils down to faith. "God loves a cheerful giver" (2 Corinthians 9:7). A gift given begrudgingly might as well not be given at all. I've come to realize that I have to let God worry about how a gift is used and let Him deal with those who take advantage of the generosity of others. It truly is a blessing to give.

Hypocrites!

What is a hypocrite anyway, instead of defining it, I'd like to share a few synonyms with you: deceit, falseness, and imitator. Are there people that fit these descriptions in church, absolutely! But there are people like this everywhere. Again, it goes back to being a matter of the heart: theirs and ours. The number of people faithfully serving the Lord far outnumbers those who are simply pretending. Okay, so much for some of the reasons not to go to church, fellowship is crucial to growth. We need to be around other Christians to help us grow.

Have you ever stopped to think why the Bible continues to be the best selling book in history? History, rules to live by, answers to everything, etc. We need to read it, we need to pray, and we need to fellowship to bring it all together. It is what being a Christian is all about, it's how we learn to be a better Christian, which is to be more like Christ.

CHOICES

6 THE CHARACTER AND NATURE OF GOD

I think one of the most important factors in changing the way people perceive God is to look at what the Bible says about the character of God. The Bible gives us many revealing details about the character and nature of God. These details paint a much different picture of Him than the image I was taught and grew up with as a child and young adult. I perceived God to be a stoic, distant, grumpy, sometimes angry, and hard to get along with, God. I pictured Him sitting in heaven waiting for people to die so He could send them to heaven or hell.

As I grew older and began to investigate for myself who God is, not only did His image change in my mind, it became much more clear to me what He is really like. I think it is crucial to understand the God we serve and to understand, as much as humanly possible, the character and nature of our Lord. This is an important part of taking God out of the box that religion places Him in.

The New Testament tells us that if we have seen Jesus we have seen the Father (John 14:9). Wow! What a wonderful blessing that is. God wanted to be able to relate to us on such a personal level that He came to dwell among us in the form of a man: Jesus. That ought to speak volumes about how much He loves us and cares about us. He stepped out of eternity and into time, as we know it, to give us a better understanding of who He is and what He expects from us.

The Bible gives us so many details about Jesus' life that it is not a difficult task to figure out what type of person he was while He lived on earth and what God the Father is like now and forever.

What is God like?

First and foremost the Bible tells us God is love. He loved us so much that He gave His only Son to be a replacement for us on Calvary's Cross. Any loving and devoted parent can easily understand how painful it was for the Lord to watch His only Son being tortured, humiliated, and them crucified. This may be why many people can't relate to or understand Him; they don't know what love is or how to recognize it when they see it. Our culture is one that is short on self-sacrifice and unconditional love. Even in Christian circles, these qualities are hard to find and these are the very places where they should be abundant. This is where many non-Christians look when they want to see and experience love. Many times all they see are people quarreling and churches splitting up because people don't know how to love each other and sacrifice for one another as God wants us to.

Does God Have a Sense of Humor?

I am a person that loves to laugh and see others laughing too. As a college instructor, I try to use humor in my classroom discussions to keep students attentive and involved. There are many examples in the Bible, in both the Old and New Testaments, where God teaches us lessons in ways that are quite humorous, especially in retrospect. We can only imagine the looks on people's faces as God, in the Old Testament, and Jesus, in the New Testament, used prophets, disciples, and miracles to teach the lessons so vital

THE CHARACTER AND NATURE OF GOD

to us even today.

There are many examples that come to mind, but one that has to rate right up there as one of the best is the occasion when Balaam's donkey spoke to him. Numbers 22-24 chronicles what happened. Balaam was a prophet on the edge. He blessed and cursed people for a price or so it seems. King Balak of Moab feared the Israelites and sent for Balaam to curse them. God told Balaam not to curse the Israelites so he sent the king's messengers on their way only to have them return to Balaam offering him more riches.

But instead of just sending them away as he should have, he again asked God what he should do. God told him to go but say only what He directed him to say. God was really giving him a choice to choose between obedience and profit but Balaam chose profit when he asked God again about what he should do. God was angry because Balaam was more focused on wealth than following His instructions so God sent an angel to kill Balaam. Balaam was unaware of the angel blocking the road prepared to strike him down but his donkey could see the angel and tried three times to avoid him. All three times Balaam beat the donkey; ignorant of the fact, she was trying to save his life.

After the third beating, God caused the donkey to speak! Can you imagine watching this! It had to be an incredible sight to see but what I find even more amazing is that Balaam was shouting back at the donkey. Then the angel asks him why he beat the donkey, as if answering to the donkey wasn't bad enough, he now has to explain his actions to the angel. That was a sight I'd have paid to see.

Some of the other Old Testament stories that come to mind are the stories of Jonah in the belly of the fish, Daniel in the lion's den, Shadrach, Meshach, and Abednego in the blazing furnace and Elijah calling down fire from heaven to name a few. Not only are these tremendous stories of faith and courage, they are also humorous. I image they weren't too funny to the people involved as these events were happening but, in retrospect, we can laugh while we learn from these lessons. Think about the many difficult situations we think are very serious at the time we were going through them; but as time passes, we can look back at what we thought to be a difficult situation and find something humorous to laugh about.

The New Testament also provides lessons in a humorous light. The cast of characters that Jesus surrounded himself with and how He handled the religious leaders of the day is laughable. Peter was impetuous to say the least. He was constantly speaking before he thought about what he was saying, something we can all relate to. Jesus was always putting Peter in his place. Then there's James and John, whom Jesus referred to as the "Sons of Thunder." Jesus' loyal followers were considered the dregs of humanity in His day. Tax collectors, lepers, and prostitutes were part of his inner circle. In fact, even His linage was full of people with questionable reputations. It's hard not to laugh when you imagine what the Sadducees and Pharisees thought of Him. He was essentially a homeless man with no possessions. Homelessness is nothing to laugh about but looking at it from the perspective that He is the Savior of all mankind... He's not what people expected.

I'm sure when the wine stopped flowing at the wedding in Galilee and Jesus performed His first recorded miracle by turning water into wine, the looks on the guest's faces must have been priceless. Even more amusing would have been the expressions on the disciple's faces' when Peter stepped out of the boat on to the surface of the water. Whether feeding thousands or healing individuals, it's impossible to know what Jesus was thinking about the reactions of those around Him in these situations but I have to believe that even though He was trying to make a point about faith, He also saw the humor in the reactions of those around Him.

Children love to laugh and have fun and the Bible tells us that children liked being close to Jesus. If Jesus didn't enjoy laughing and having a good time it is unlikely that children would have wanted to be around Him. Jesus said, speaking metaphorically of us as His sheep (followers), "I have come that they may have life, and have it to the full" (John 10:10), and life is not full without laughter.

What else does God's word say about His nature?

It speaks of His jealousy, anger, justice, and wrath, but more importantly, it speaks of His compassion, grace, and mercy. Naysayers point to His anger, jealousy, and wrath and ask why they should worship a God like that. What they fail to realize is that if they searched the scriptures in reference to these characteristics, they would find that He is slow to anger and is fair in justice. They would also see that His jealousy is in relationship to His love for us. These characteristics are taken out of context many times. If we are being honest about the nature of humans, we would realize that we all deserve God's wrath, but because He loves us so much, we are more likely to experience His compassion, grace, and mercy.

Rick Warren says, in respect to God's love, "He gives you many evidences: God says He loves you; you're never out of His sight; He cares about every detail of your life; He gave you the capacity to enjoy all kinds of pleasure; He has good plans for your life; He forgives you; and He is lovingly patient with you. God loves you infinitely more than you can imagine."[1] Well said.

If God didn't care about us, He wouldn't have sent Jesus to die in our place but He did. Countless times in the Old Testament, God gave the Israelites the opportunity to turn from their vile ways of practicing idol worship and worship Him; and, countless times, they rejected Him. Only after repeated offenses did God respond in a negative way. The Lord wants us to fellowship with Him. He wants a relationship with us, an intimate relationship. He is waiting to show His compassion and mercy to anyone who asks. What kind of God do we serve? God is AWESOME and LOVING!

7 RELIGION OR RELATIONSHIP

Religious arrogance is nothing new; neither is misguided teaching. Paul warned of it in the first century. "See to it that no one takes you captive through hollow and deceptive philosophy, which depends on human tradition and the basic principles of this world rather than on Christ" (Colossians 2:8). Religious people are very good at pointing out how well they follow the rules of the church. They also make it very clear who doesn't. What they fail to realize is that they are only condemning themselves. Legalists (those who follow these rules, biblical or not) usually are not very good imitators of Christ. Their accusatory attitude is just one example of how they are not imitating Christ. They point out the failings of others to divert attention from their own shortcomings. But this is also nothing new as the following scripture passage illustrates.

> The Pharisees and some of the teachers of the law who had come from Jerusalem gathered around Jesus and saw some of his disciples eating food with hands that were "unclean," that is, unwashed. (The Pharisees and all the Jews did not eat unless they gave their hands a ceremonial washing, holding to the tradition of the elders. When they come from the marketplace they did not eat unless they washed. They observed many other traditions, such as the

washing of cups, pitchers and kettles.)

So the Pharisees and teachers of the law asked Jesus, "Why don't your disciples live according to the tradition of the elders instead of eating their food with `unclean' hands?" He replied, "Isaiah was right when he prophesied about you hypocrites; as it is written: 'These people honor me with their lips, but their hearts are far from me. They worship me in vain; their teachings are but rules taught by men.' You have let go of the commands of God and are holding on to the traditions of men." And he said to them: "You have a fine way of setting aside the commands of God in order to observe your own traditions" (Mark 7:1-9).

I think it is safe to say that Jesus did not like the behavior of the religious leaders of biblical times. There are countless examples, other than the one above, that illustrate this fact. In fact, it is my experience that religious people generally aren't very effective in leading others to Christ because nobody wants to be around them. They tend to be pompous and judgmental. Every Christian that I have ever known to be an effective soul winner for God is not a religious person at all. They are Christ-like. They strive to treat others as Christ treats them. They don't act like they are better than or, in some way, above others. They simply try to practice what they believe. Christianity is a relationship not a religion. Christians should be practicing relationships with others the way they do with Jesus.

Jesus was quoting Isaiah in the verse above but given that all scripture is God breathed, He was speaking for Himself when He said of the Pharisees, "their teachings are but rules taught by men." I have attended many churches all over the world and in some of them I wondered if they even knew the Bible existed! They did and said things in the services that have no biblical basis at all that I'm aware of. It is very noticeable in these churches that the people lack the joy that should be part of their worship experience. They are like robots going through useless religious rituals.

In Isaiah 29 God complains about redundant religious exercise. Their worship was not sincere and their actions were hypocritical. They were more concerned with their religion than they were with their relationship with the Lord. The same is true of many churches today. What's worse is many people in these churches tend to be very judgmental of those who do not subscribe to their form of worship or beliefs.

Even in Bible teaching churches, some people become more concerned about the format of worship or the music or even the length of the service then they are about heart-felt worship. More than one church has split apart over senseless bickering about religious exercise. People visiting churches like this usually only visit once and after visiting a couple more places like that, they don't see any point in going back to church at all. They can experience bickering, hidden agendas, dishonesty, judgmental attitudes and self-ishness at home, work, or where they socialize. God wants us to worship Him with passionate joy and commitment, not ritual and tradition.

When people go to church for the first time or especially after a long hiatus, they are usually looking for something they can't find anywhere else; they're looking for acceptance, compassion, and love. The last thing they want is someone criticizing them for how they look or what their present life-style is, if it's known. I have found that one of the quickest ways to turn a person away from Christ is to treat them judgmentally.

When we are honest with God, it strengthens our relationship with Him. During times in my life when I struggled with adversity and didn't understand why, it seemed to me that God was ignoring my pleas for help. I became angry. I would yell when I prayed; not to be disrespectful, but out of frustration. It was during those episodes that God seemed to whisper to me and make a point about my circumstance. I was speaking from my heart and God responded.

Rick Warren sums up being honest with God like this, he says, "Can God handle that kind of frank, intense honesty from you? Absolutely! Genuine friendship is built on disclosure. What may appear as audacity, God views as authenticity. God listens to the passionate words of His friends; He is bored with predictable, pious clichés. To be God's friend, you must be honest to God, sharing your true feeling, not what you think you ought to feel or say."[1] Honesty is arguably the most important element in a relationship, especially in our relationship with God.

Legalism (being religious) is nothing new, as mentioned earlier, God was unhappy because of the Israelites empty worship rituals and only a few short years after Jesus' ascension, the disciples had to get together in Jerusalem to deal with the same thing! Christianity was only a few years old and legalism was already a problem, God wants us to be honest with Him. He wants us to be genuine. God wants us to call Him Father; He wants to be our friend. He wants us to enjoy a personal relationship with him not a religious experience.

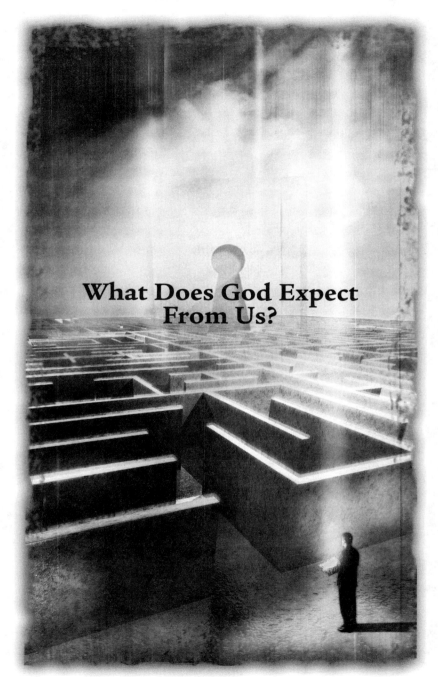

What Does God Expect From Us?

CHOICES

8 BE AN EXAMPLE

Every Christian should strive to be like Jesus in every way. The Bible is very clear about what God expects of us. We know we'll never be perfect and it is a fool that believes they are perfect. However, every day our prayer should be to be more like Jesus. The Bible says, "God is love" (1 John 4:8). It sounds like an oversimplification, but if we all loved each other the way God loves us, there would be peace in the world. Jesus instructs us to love our enemies; that's a tall order. How do you love your enemies? I thought there was no way in the world to do this. This was an unrealistic expectation.

Can it really be that simple? In a word, yes! According to the world's point of view, we should get even, or not tolerate mistreatment from anyone. We should stand our ground and the like. The Bible and Jesus teach the contrary. Jesus says, "Do not resist an evil person. If someone strikes you on the right cheek, turn to him the other also" (Matthew 5:39). "You have heard that it was said, `Love your neighbor and hate your enemy.' But I tell you: Love your enemies and pray for those who persecute you" (Matthew 5:43-44). Does this imply we must all be doormats to be good Christians? Absolutely not! Jesus is telling us to use kindness to defuse a bad situation and I can say from personal experience, it works!

People expect retaliation in response to aggressive or

offensive behavior. When we act with compassion, people are caught off guard. How do you respond when you are expecting an angry or defensive response but get just the opposite? Sometimes people may react more aggressively, feeling they are dealing with a weak opponent or they'll feel guilty because of the kindness they receive. But, I've discovered by being kind in situations I may not have been in the past, most of the time, the person reciprocates in kind.

People feel compelled to make sure they get even for grievous acts against them. But again, the Bible tells us just the opposite, "Do not take revenge, my friends, but leave room for God's wrath, for it is written: 'It is mine to avenge; I will repay,' says the Lord" (Romans 12:19). In fact, the Lord takes it a step further when He says, "If your enemy is hungry, feed him; if he is thirsty, give him something to drink. In doing this, you will heap burning coals on his head" (Romans 12:20). If your motive is heaping burning coals on their head, you're defeating the purpose.

As I'm writing this, the second war in Iraq is unfolding. Many reports from journalists imbedded with coalition troops capture the images of soldiers and marines showing compassion for the enemy. Captured prisoners of war receive food, water, blankets, and when needed, medical attention. These are man showing great compassion to those that, moments before, were trying to kill them. What makes this type of treatment possible is the compassion of the coalition forces. They are being empathetic. They realize that many of the Iraqi's that are fighting against them do not want to be there. They are there because of coercion. In fact, many surrender because they know the enemy, the coalition forces, will treat them better than their own government. We can actually gain alliances with kindness. I think that's the point the Lord is trying to make. Win a friend instead of gaining an enemy by demonstrating compassion and kindness.

A person that doesn't have a personal relationship with Christ and even some that do, find this very difficult to do. We can't act like Christ until He becomes a welcomed part of our life. Many non-Christians are very kind and compassionate; but, to be true imitators of Jesus, we must receive the fruits of the Spirit and to receive the fruits we must first receive the Spirit. What are those fruits, "the fruit of the Spirit is love, joy, peace, patience, kindness, goodness, faithfulness, gentleness and self-control. Against such things there is no law" (Galatians 5:22-23).

I volunteer at the local jail to teach the gospel and counsel with inmates. I ask inmates on a weekly basis if they have ever had anyone upset with them for displaying these characteristics (the fruits of the Spirit). If we responded to others with the fruits of the Spirit instead of how the world expects us to respond, interpersonal conflict would be unheard of.

These are men easily forgotten by our society. They are seen as lost causes and are getting what they deserve. If God looked at us in the same light, we'd all be on our way to Hell. As I talk with the prisoners, I try to remember that. It keeps me humble. When individuals feel they are above anyone else for any reason they are in danger of judgment themselves. They are also deceiving themselves. Paul makes this very clear when he says, "If anyone thinks he is something when he is nothing, he deceives himself. Each one should test his own actions" (Galatians 6:3-4). If you want to compare yourself to someone, make it Jesus.

Loving others as God loves us is the best example we can set for others to follow; but we should be examples in other areas too. Witnessing, tithing, and service are just a few of the ways we can influence others for Christ. I can speak about each of these from a personal point of view. Each of these areas is very important and when practiced as the Lord instructs, can have significant influence in leading others to Jesus. It also strengthens our personal relationship with the Lord. There is an indescribable joy in having a person want to accept Christ because of what they see in your life and how you treat others. This is an open invitation to witness to that person about Jesus. They approach you based on what they've seen in you: Christ. In this way, I feel we are being the salt and the light of our world as the Bible instructs us. People are thirsty for what we have in our life (Jesus) and we now have an open door to show them the way to Him.

Witnessing to Others

Witnessing can be a double-edged sword. Done properly, it can be very effective in winning people to Christ. Sometimes the best way to witness is with our actions, as mentioned previously. It's easy to profess to what you believe; it's quite another to put your beliefs into practice. It goes back to the old, but very true, cliché; actions speak louder than words. People want to see what Christ is doing in your life more than they want to hear about it.

Overzealous witnesses can turn people away from Jesus as fast as anything else you can think of. Their excitement may be well intentioned and very sincere but hitting people over the head with the Bible is an ineffective way to witness to others. Jesus gives us the perfect example. He never forced Himself or His views on others. He answered questions when asked and used teaching opportunities to spread God's word. He was usually very subtle and always factual. When He quoted scripture, it was word for word and not taken out of context.

Let your life do the talking. Love those that are unlovable. When asked about why nothing seems to get you down, take the time to give God the credit. Watching how my grandpa ran his business, treats his family, and faithfully worships and serves God speaks volumes about his relationship with the Lord. He never fails to witness to others when the door is open but he never kicks the door down and forces his way in either.

Tithing

Tithing is an area that causes much trepidation among believers and non-believers. I mentioned this earlier when I spoke of the verse in Malachi when God speaks of believers robbing Him by not tithing. I was guilty of robbing God. I can think of two reasons why I was doing this. The first was ignorance, ignorance about what tithing is and why God expects us to tithe. The second was two-fold, selfishness and lack of faith.

Ignorance is a weak excuse for anything. The Bible tells us what we need to know if we open it up and look for answers. (Mentoring is also a good way to overcome ignorance discussed in another chapter.) Many people don't stop to think that one of the reasons the Lord directs us to tithe is to support His servants. Pastors need to support their families just like the rest of us and they depend on those attending their church for that support. We also need to support the facilities we worship in. God directs us to tithe but more so, He expects us to tithe with a joyful heart to support those that serve Him.

Many people are also unaware of the missions and missionaries that their local church supports. These servants of the Lord are usually responsible for raising the funds necessary to support their ministry as well as perform the service they are called to do. The support they receive from local congregations allows them to focus more attention on their mission. God tells us to store up treasures in heaven. When we tithe it's like putting money in your heavenly bank account and the interest rate is out of this world...

Selfishness and lack of faith are more difficult obstacles to overcome. First, most of us don't get really excited about giving our money away unless it's for lottery tickets or casino excursions. When a tax proposal for schools is on the ballot that would increase an individuals taxes a couple dollars a month for the benefit of the children in the community, people raise a fuss about the prospect of their taxes going up even for a worthy cause. But tell a person that they have a chance to win a million dollars, even when the odds of doing so are astronomical, and they'll give their money away hand over fist.

Lack of faith is another reason I struggled with tithing. I didn't see any way I could pay my bills and care for my family after giving a tenth of my income to the Lord. I've heard many people testify to the fact that, at some time in their spiritual growth process, they felt convicted about tithing so they just decided to do it. (It's definitely a huge leap of faith.) They report that after they began tithing, they always had enough to take care of all their obligations and still had money to spare. I would think to myself yea, right... until I felt convicted to do the same and experienced what they were talking about myself!

Money is not a bad thing but the Bible warns that it can be if it becomes our focus and motivation. "No one can serve two masters. Either he will hate the one and love the other, or he will be devoted to the one and despise the other. You cannot serve both God and Money" (Matthew 6:24).

One of the most misquoted verses of scripture is 1 Timothy 6:10. Many people will tell you the Bible says money is the root of all evil when it actually says, "the **love of money** is a root of all kinds of evil." (Emphasis added). It's all God's to begin with and He only asks for a little back to further His kingdom by supporting those that faithfully serve Him. That's why He goes on to tell us "Do not store up for yourselves treasures on earth, where moth and rust destroy, and where thieves break in and steal. But store up for yourselves treasures in heaven, where moth and rust do not destroy, and where thieves do not break in and steal" (Matthew 6:19-20). It's all about priorities, are yours earthly or heavenly? God will always make sure we have what we need if we trust Him.

God illustrates His concern for our needs and speaks specifically of faith when He says, "Therefore I tell you, do not worry about your life, what you will eat or drink; or about your body, what you will wear. Is not life more important than food, and the body more important than clothes? Look at the birds of the air; they do not sow or reap or store away in barns, and yet your heavenly Father feeds them. Are you not much more valuable than they? Who of you by worrying can add a single hour to his life? "And why do you worry about clothes? See how the lilies of the field grow. They do not labor or spin. Yet I tell you that not even Solomon in all his splendor was dressed like one of these. If that is how God clothes the grass of the field, which is here today and tomorrow is thrown into the fire, will he not much more clothe you, O you of little faith" (Matthew 6:25-30)?

Selfishness is tough to overcome but it can be with patience and prayer. When I began tithing and trusting God to meet my needs, I found out first-hand that the Lord was serious when He says, "test me on this!" I make less now than I have in the past several years, yet I'm as financially comfortable as I've ever been in me life while giving more to charity than ever before. This brings up another point about tithing.

People debate what is God's work? Is it just the church and missions or other charities? do you tithe on net or gross pay? If God is glorified in some way and His kingdom benefits then you are giving to the Lord. Praying helps. God convicts us if we need to reconsider how we give. People also debate if God expects us to tithe from our net or gross pay. The Bible is very clear about this, "As soon as the order went out, the Israelites generously gave the first fruits of their grain, new wine, oil and honey and all that the fields produced. They brought a great amount, a tithe of everything" (2 Chronicles 31:5). If you are unsure, pray about it.

Many people are reluctant to give because of the charlatans they see that preach God's word and live like the devil. They justify not giving because they perceive that everyone in on the take. There are many charities of late that have come under fire due to mismanagement of contributions. We must continue to give to help the less fortunate and let the law, and the Lord, deal with those that are profiting from others generosity. The same is true for contributing to the church.

There are some people who preach for profit. Their heart is in the wrong place but the irony is that God's word never returns void. It's not for us to decide if the Lord's servants are deceivers or not. That's God's job. If we were suspicious of everyone involved with non-profit organizations, many needy people would never get help. There are many needy souls in the world and tithing helps support the ministries that are trying to reach them. Step out in faith and let God sort out the rest; He'll amaze you!

Service

Service is another area we can be an example to others. In fact, this is a crucial part of being an effective witness for Christ. We should have a desire to share the good news and the peace that God brings to our life with those around us. When the fruits of the Spirit are obvious in our actions, we glorify God. We can serve the Lord in many different ways through several different agencies using the gifts God blessed us with. You don't have to be an expert at something to help others. God looks at the heart and appreciates our effort. He will provide whatever we need to get the job done if our heart is in it. Recently someone told me that God doesn't call the qualified; He qualifies the called. How true!

The Bible makes this very clear; "there are different kinds of service, but the same Lord. There are different kinds of working, but the same God works all of them in all men. Now to each one the manifestation of the Spirit is given for the common good. To one there is given through the Spirit the message of wisdom, to another the message of knowledge by means of the same Spirit, to another faith by the same Spirit, to another gifts of healing by that one Spirit, to another miraculous powers, to another prophecy, to another distinguishing between spirits, to another speaking in different kinds of tongues, and to still another the interpretation of tongues. All these are the work of one and the same Spirit, and he gives them to each one, just as he determines. The body is a unit, though it is made up of many parts; and though all its parts are many, they form one body. So it is with Christ"

(1 Corinthians 12:5-12). Offer yourself for service and the Lord will use you.

Rick Warren stresses the importance of service and a servant's heart. He points out, according to the Bible, that we are created, saved, called, and commanded to serve God. He also points out that our natural inclination to be selfish is in direct opposition of serving God and others. But the importance of service cannot be understated in regard to setting an example for others to follow.[1]

Having a servant's heart is an essential part of our relationship with the Lord. Jesus exemplified this through word and deed. In word He says, "For even the Son of Man did not come to be served, but to serve, and to give his life as a ransom for many" (Mark 10:45). And, "I am among you as one who serves" (Luke 22:27). In deed, "Now that I, your Lord and Teacher, have washed your feet, you also should wash one another's feet. I have set you an example that you should do as I have done for you" (John 13:14-15). And His greatest act of service was His death on the cross providing a way for our reconciliation with God. If we want to be Christ-like, we must be willing to serve others in a sacrificial way, not just when it's convenient or when we have some extra time or money, but with a servant's heart.

How important is our service to the Lord? He tells us "To love him with all your heart, with all your understanding and with all your strength, and to love your neighbor as yourself is more important than all burnt offerings and sacrifices" (Mark 12:33). We demonstrate our love for Him by our actions through our service to Him.

These are but a few ways we can be good examples to those around us. God doesn't just expect us to be good examples, He commands that we are and with the power of the Holy Spirit, we can be.

God also commands us to leave judgment up to Him. A judgmental person is a non-example of Christ-like behavior. You can be a great example in every aspect of your life, but being unforgiving and thinking yourself better than someone else will hamper your testimony for Jesus. That is the subject of the next section.

9 JUDGE NOT

It always amazes me how fast people are to point out the flaws of those around them. They seem to forget about the three fingers that are pointing back at them. One reason we are so good at finding the faults of others is that we're usually guilty of the same offense(s). We like to point out those we feel are greater offenders than we are to take some of the heat off ourselves. Paul tells us in Galatians not to compare ourselves with others but look at our own motives, test our own actions.

Our job should be leading people to Christ through love and compassion regardless of their past or present circumstances. It is not for us to concern ourselves with what people have done or what their present convictions might be, that's God's concern. He will reveal to them, in His time, what He thinks they should or shouldn't do. It is our responsibility to rebuke in a compassionate way. But we must be sure that the rebuke is biblically based and not of our own convictions.

Two examples come to mind when I think of how judgmental attitudes can cast a shadow on Christianity. In the late 1980's and again in the late 1990's, representatives of the religious right made very inflammatory public statements. The first was about a film made about Jesus and the other was in regard to a television celebrity that made her homosexual lifestyle public. What's worse is many people look at these "Christian leaders" as speaking for all

Christians everywhere!

In the first case, a film called "The Last Temptation of Christ" received severe criticism from many religious leaders because they considered it blasphemous. At the time, I remember hearing comments about how the movie portrayed Jesus having sex with Mary Magdalene and that many of the other scenes were not biblically sound. I remember thinking how disgusted I was that someone would make a movie like that and vowed not to watch it. I didn't, until ten years later.

Shortly after I arrived at Kunsan Air Base in South Korea, I was at the recreation center, one evening, looking into the activities available there. They had a video rental section so I started looking through the selections and came across this movie. Honestly, up to this point, I'd never even seen it available for rent, but I wasn't really looking for it either. My curiosity got the best of me. I wanted to see for myself what was so horrible about this film and I rented the video. I told myself to have an open mind about the story line to try to understand the director's motivation.

At the very beginning of the film there was a disclaimer that says the film is not based on scripture but that it's a layman's attempt to explore and understand Jesus' motivation for doing what He did. As I watched the film, there were some aspects of it that made me a little uncomfortable at first but then I tried to imagine how a person that had never been in a church, or had very limited exposure to the gospel, might perceive Jesus and the temptations He faced, especially knowing that He had the power of God at His fingertips.

There were some very interesting points of view depicted in the film that were a big departure from the paradigms that I grew up with in a religious environment. The first one that comes to mind is Judas walking into the shop where

Jesus and His father work as carpenters. Judas has just finished fighting with some Roman soldiers because of their attempts to oppress the people of Israel. When he walks into the woodshop he finds Jesus making crosses for the Romans. Though probably not true, it makes you think.

Another scene depicts Jesus walking into a brothel. I was ready to turn the film off because I was not going to watch any more if what I thought was about to happen did; but it didn't. After everyone left and only Mary Magdalene and Jesus remained, He approaches her and even though she attempts to seduce Him, He declines her advances. She is obviously upset with Him and He asked for forgiveness. Again, I'm wondering where this was going and why He would be asking for her forgiveness. What happened next really struck a chord with me.

You get the sense from their conversation, that they were childhood friends and grew up together. It's also obvious that Mary wanted to be more than friends with Jesus. He was asking for her forgiveness because He felt like He was hurting her by not wanting to marry her. He knew what His mission was and that His mission didn't include a wife. This really struck me because it brought Jesus' humanity closer to home. We seem to have no problem thinking of Jesus as God in the flesh but we sometimes forget that He was flesh. He loves us so much that He put Himself in our shoes. We can't say He doesn't understand or know how we feel; He knows exactly how we feel. This scene made that very clear. He had to deal with all the feelings and emotions we do.

The part of the movie that really seemed to pinch the religious right was a scene after He was crucified. In the midst of His suffering on the cross, a little girl approaches the cross. She proceeds to tell Him that His Father is well pleased with Him because He was willing to die for the people of the world and now that he demonstrated that willingness to follow God's will, no matter the cost, there was no need to die. (Anyone that knows the story of Abraham would not find this too hard to believe. God spared his beloved son after Abraham demonstrated his willingness to obey God even to the point of sacrificing his own son.) She proceeds to pull the nails from His feet and hands and cleans His wounds, and then they begin walking toward a nearby village.

As they approached the village, they come upon a wedding party and Jesus asks who is getting married. The girl said you are. Mary Magdalene was waiting for Jesus to arrive so they could marry. After they wed, you are led to believe they consummate their marriage, not in a graphic way by any means. I found nothing offensive about this because they were married! Others are still preaching His death and resurrection seeming to ignore the fact he's still alive and among them. He has many children and grows to be an old man. Then, on his deathbed, the story takes a dramatic turn.

As Jesus lay dying, His disciples gather around Him. He asks to see Judas, to which John replies, "He may not come, he's still very angry." The movie portrays Judas and Jesus as life-long friends, and Jesus asks Judas to turn Him over to the Pharisees because He knew nobody else would be strong enough to do it. Judas reluctantly agrees. This is not biblical but it sets the stage for what is about to happen as Jesus lay dying.

Judas does show up and he's very angry because He turned his best friend over to the Pharisees to die and for what? Jesus then tries to crawl from the house saying I belong on the cross, I need to be there, I want to be there and in an instant He's back on the cross. What an image! Being God, He could have come down from the cross, He didn't have to be there and Satan knew it. He had to be there because He wanted to be. I don't think it was a reach to imagine that Jesus may have thought, on occasion, what it would be like to have a family of His own, especially as He suffered on the cross. He loved kids, and He loved being around people. Satan didn't want Him there; this was the last temptation... I felt more love for the Lord after watching this film because I felt, more than ever before, that He understood me better than I ever dreamed He could. It made me appreciate even more that He was without sin even though He was human.

I must admit that this movie might be difficult for some to watch but I saw nothing blasphemous about it. It presented a different point of view and it gets people thinking outside the box in regard to the temptation Jesus faced as a human. The two big problems I see with the reaction of the religious right to this movie is that, first, it was an opportunity lost. This could have been a great way to get Christians and non-Christians talking about the truths of scripture versus the account depicted in the movie. Second, it was an over-reaction that made Christians look pompous and self-righteous, distancing themselves from the ones they should be reaching out to.

The second example of how judgmental attitudes damage our witness was when a well-known television personality made a public profession of her homosexuality. After confessing she was gay, there were many people voicing their opinion about the incident both for and against. One person voicing his opinion was a person that is quoted many times as speaking for the religious right. He made a public statement calling the television celebrity names in reference to her sexual preference.

It is our responsibility to assure people know and understand what the Bible says about issues like homosexuality but I don't think God intends for us to be abusive in the process. How is that going to encourage someone to reconsider his or her position? I thought about what Jesus might do and I really couldn't imagine Jesus making an abusive comment. Can you imagine the scene when the adulterous woman was brought before Jesus and Jesus saying, "You without sin stone the whore?" I can't. We're much more likely to persuade people to give their life to Christ by showing them compassion and kindness versus sarcasm and a judgmental attitude.

We need to focus on our relationship with the Lord. The only question that is important to answer is, does Jesus approve of my action or decision? If we can honestly answer that question in a positive way based on biblical truths then we needn't concern ourselves with what others might think or say or do. Joshua sums up service and doing what the Lord desires us to do in a very simple statement, "But as for me and my household, we will serve the LORD" (Joshua 24:15). What God will you serve? What choices will you make?

10 MENTORING A NEW BELIEVER

What is mentoring and why is it important? Mentoring is teaching, training, instructing, guiding and/or advising an individual or group. Overcoming ignorance is one of the most important reasons for mentoring new believers. Two Bible passages come to mind that point to the necessity to instruct others in the word, especially new believers. The first is the parable of the farmer sowing his seed. "A farmer went out to sow his seed. As he was scattering the seed, some fell along the path, and the birds came and ate it up. Some fell on rocky places, where it did not have much soil. It sprang up quickly, because the soil was shallow. But when the sun came up, the plants were scorched, and they withered because they had no root. Other seed fell among thorns, which grew up and choked the plants. Still other seed fell on good soil, where it produced a crop--a hundred, sixty or thirty times what was sown" (Matthew 13:3-8).

When Jesus disciples ask Him what the story means, He tells them, "When anyone hears the message about the kingdom and does not understand it, the evil one comes and snatches away what was sown in his heart. This is the seed sown along the path. The one who received the seed that fell on rocky places is the man who hears the word and at once receives it with joy. But since he has no root, he lasts only a short time. When trouble or persecution comes because of the word, he quickly falls away. The one who received the seed that fell among the thorns is the man who hears the word, but the worries of this life and the deceitfulness of wealth choke it, making it unfruitful. But the one who received the seed that fell on good soil is the man who hears the word and understands it. He produces a crop, yielding a hundred, sixty or thirty times what was sown" (Matthew 13:19-23).

How many new Christians fall victim to what Jesus is talking about in this parable. I would contend that many who fall away from God for the reasons described in this parable fall victim to Satan for a lack of mentoring. The first problem Jesus identifies is a lack of understanding. This is clearly a problem in teaching. When someone receives the word with great joy but falls away quickly in times of trouble and the person that is choked out by the worries of the world or worldly possessions would indicate a lack of support that a mentor and the church can provide. That's not to say that even with Christian love, teaching, and support that the world won't somehow overcome the word, but I think many fall victim to Satan's schemes much faster because they lack guidance.

Earlier I spoke of a good friend I had the privilege of praying with to accept Christ as his Savior. I also mentioned the phone calls in the middle of the night to answer questions he had about what he read in the Bible. It was exciting for me to see him searching God's word for answers and a thrill to know I may be able to help him understand God's word and maintain his excitement. I try to make myself as available as possible to anyone that is trying to learn more about the Lord. I know there are many people I can count on, at any time, to answer my questions or concerns and this is a real comfort for me.

The other verse of scripture that comes to mind is Paul's comment's to the Corinthians about their spiritual progress or lack of it when he says, "Brothers, I could not address you as spiritual but as worldly—mere infants in Christ. I gave you milk, not solid food, for you were not yet ready for it. Indeed, you are still not ready. You are still worldly. For since there is jealousy and quarreling among you, are you not worldly? Are you not acting like mere men" (1 Corinthians 3:1-3). New Christians are not the only group that can benefit from mentoring, some people that profess Christ as their Lord and Savior go through the motions of faith in Christ but do not enjoy a true relationship with Him. They never really grow to reap all the benefits that a growing relationship with the Lord can offer. Some may continue to practice their religion for years and never get past the babes in Christ stage, others simply fall away from Christ because they really can't see the point in following Him; their life remains unchanged.

Without instruction, many believers remain babes in Christ and they are more likely to be led astray without guidance. Mature Christians, must do whatever they can to facilitate the growth of new believers to help keep them from falling victim to an apathetic world. The complete absence of a mentor usually speeds up the process. A mentor is most helpful when a person has a desire to know Christ better. All the mentoring in the world is only as good as the desire that an individual has to grow in Christ. It's still an individual responsibility. That is the focus of the next section.

It's important that we take the responsibility to ensure that we are doing what we can to strengthen our relationship with the Lord. By doing so, we are better capable to deal with the trouble that we face in our daily lives. Not because we are any more capable of handling things on our own, but because of the strength we have in Jesus. "My grace is sufficient for you, for my power is made perfect in weakness" (2 Corinthians 12:9). When we are close to God, we seek the truth; and, when we seek the truth we tend to be much more honest with ourselves... Our weaknesses become more evident.

When we are honest with ourselves, we are less likely to deceive ourselves or the people around us. We do not put up facades or make excuses for unacceptable behavior. We own up to our shortcomings and hold ourselves accountable for our actions. We seek out people that will hold us accountable as well. We have nothing to hide. When we have nothing to hide, we tend to feel more at ease and less conflicted emotionally. But the true measure of a person is not how they act when others are around, but rather how they act when nobody is around, except Jesus. And we are all accountable to Him.

11 PERSONAL RESPONSIBILITY

Modern Psychology would have us believe there is a good reason (excuse) why people behave poorly and that if we have behavioral and emotional problems the solution is as close as the local psychologist, psychiatrist, or pharmacist. Many times counseling becomes a futile effort for both the counselor and the person receiving the guidance because people are looking for somebody to blame instead of being accountable for their own actions. There are several commercials advertising all the different drugs that can help us to be our "old self" again, really? What does this imply to our children? We tell them drugs are dangerous and yet advertise them as a way to help us feel normal.

What ever happened to personal responsibility? Our society has become one that advocates blaming others for our own self-inflicted misery. Jay Adams speaks of O. Hobart Mower's antithetically proposed Moral Model of responsibility. He says, "The "patient's" problems are moral, not medical. He suffers from real guilt, not guilt feelings (false guilt). The basic irregularity is not emotional but behavioral. He is not a victim of his conscience, but a violator of it. He must stop blaming others and accept responsibility for his own poor behavior. Problems may be solved, not by ventilation of feelings, but rather confession of sin." [1]

We live in a society that allows a person to bring a multimillion dollar lawsuit against a fast food company for burning themselves with a hot cup of coffee or because children are overweight from poor eating habits. It's no wonder then, that when people are guilty of heinous crimes, they look to blame someone else or some condition never known before, until it is brought up in a defense strategy that allows a guilty person to not have to deal with the consequences of their behavior.

I see it every week when I go down to the county jail to counsel with inmates. As I speak of accountability and poor choices, many know that their predicament is of their own doing. Whether they own up to it in court is a different story. What happened to justice? I thought justice was assuring that innocent people remained free while those that are guilty suffer the consequences of their actions. Now it seems that integrity is just a word. If a person has enough money or there is fame to be won by defending a person regardless of their guilt or innocence that's all that matters: how sad.

As mentioned earlier, the Bible is often misquoted on the subject of money and its' effect on people; many say, "The Bible says that money is the root of all evil." It actually says the love of money is the problem. What's this got to do with the subject of behavioral and emotional problems? Isn't it obvious? Why are most crimes committed: selfishness, greed, and jealousy. These are the same issues that cause us to be deceitful contributing to feelings of inadequacy and failure.

The Bible is also very specific about what happens to someone who allows these attitudes to control him or her. In Galatians, the Apostle Paul says, "The acts of the sinful nature are obvious: sexual immorality, impurity and debauchery; idolatry and witchcraft; hatred, discord, jealousy, fits of rage, selfish ambition, dissensions, factions and envy; drunkenness, orgies, and the like. I warn you, as I did before, that those who live like this will not inherit the kingdom of God" (Galatians 5:19-21). This doesn't describe a mental condition; it describes selfishness. Adams was right, we violate our conscience then try to justify our actions knowing in our heart, we are wrong.

At this point I want to make something very clear. As the parent of a child that suffers from learning disabilities that escape diagnosis, I understand that there are very real organically based psychological problems that people suffer from. Modern technology is allowing us to see the brain in ways never thought possible even ten years ago, but are people receiving the proper tests before the diagnosis of a chemical imbalance and prescribed drugs to correct the problem? The over diagnosis of disorders like Attention Deficit Disorder (A.D.D.) for example, would indicate that every child that misbehaves in school is suffering from this disease and requires medication. The same can be said for those that advocate drugs to help us feel normal!

I also want to make it very clear that I don't have the answers nor will I pretend that I do, but as I continue to grow in my relationship with Christ and search the scriptures for guidance, direction, and comfort, the more I realize that God's word addresses everything that we need to know about any issue. It does have all the answers if we're willing to look for them. We do this by searching God's word for the answers.

12 FINDING THE ANSWERS

Searching the scriptures is much more than a cursory look at the Bible of even reading it through from beginning to end. A person must try to understand the historical and social context of the time the author wrote the book as well as how it applies to us today. People must try to understand that the Greek and Hebrew languages are difficult to translate into English therefore searching may include reading different translations of the Bible to fully understand the meaning. Some may say this is a daunting and arduous task to understand God's direction, however it truly becomes a labor of love for those searching for truth. In my own search, I find it very helpful to read the perspectives of others in regard to scripture along with various translations. When combined with prayer, God is very faithful in providing understanding.

People seem surprised and even shocked at the things they see and hear in the news like what they're hearing has never been done before; how could anyone stoop to these levels? But as you read and study history you find that horrible human behavior is nothing new and, in fact, the behavior prevalent in antiquity is as, if not more, horrible than anything we see in the world today. So why don't more people study the Bible? That question can be answered in a word: religion.

Religion has arguably turned more people away from

God and the Bible than anything else. Some religions go as far as encouraging their followers not to read it: let the leaders read it and interpret it. Much of this is due to ignorance. When we know little of a subject, we tend to take people at their word if we feel they are more knowledgeable or qualified about it. This leads many people away from Christ, because of men trying to "help" God out. This is a best-case scenario; at other times selfishness and greed are motivators to compromise God's word. As a child, I grew up being told of many things the Bible did or didn't say only to find out through my own research what is really written between its cover.

It is not an accident however, that religion turns people away from God. Satan uses this tactic and has been for countless millennium. The Bible tells us of Jesus' disdain for religion. When the Bible speaks of the church, it speaks of us being brothers and sisters in Christ, following God's word, not adhering to a bunch of man-made rules or poor, self-indulging interpretations of God's word. Not only can these man-made rules be impractical, they can be impossible to follow leading people into sin and away from salvation.

When we search the scriptures, God reveals to us the truth about Himself and what He wants for us in this life and our life with Him in eternity. The intent of this book is to emphasis the importance of reading the Bible to find the answers to the questions we so often ask about the nature of God, life and how to live it, and where we fit into the picture. The answers are there if we are only willing to look, but we must look with the mind and heart of Christ. The Bible tells us "The man without the Spirit does not accept the things that come from the Spirit of God, for they are foolishness to him, and he cannot understand them, because they are spiritually discerned" (1 Corinthians 2:14).

FINDING THE ANSWERS 115

Like I said earlier, we are accountable to God. Anyone that hears the gospel and rejects it, rejects God. We will all have to answer to that question one day, what will your answer be? God, in His grace and mercy, also makes this simple for us. All we have to do is pray to accept Jesus as our Savior and Redeemer and invite Him into our heart to be the Lord of our life. There are no magic words or phrases, just a simple acknowledgement and invitation with a sincere heart is all it takes to become a child of God. He will do the rest if you let Him.

Countless people, myself included, wait for the world to bring us to our knees before we ask for God's help. We blame everyone else for our unhappiness. George Bernard Shaw wrote, "This is the true joy of life: the being used up for a purpose recognized by yourself as a mighty one; being a force of nature instead of a feverish, selfish little clot of ailments and grievances, complaining that the world will not devote itself to making you happy." We are the only people that can make us happy and we can't do it by ourselves. God wants to carry our burdens and lighten our load. Don't let the weight of the world bring you to your knees, do it on your own. Confess your sin and take responsibility for your actions and He is quick to forgive. When He takes our burdens He sets us free. Sooner or later we all come to realize that God succeeds when everything else fails.

116 CHOICES

13 QUESTIONS OR EXCUSES

Why do some people avoid going to church? As mentioned before, it may be do to feeling unwelcome or because of hypocritical attitudes. Some struggle with questions about God; questions that mentoring can help answer. But are these questions that people are sincerely seeking answers to or just excuses to not attend church or have a relationship with the Lord? What follows are a few of these questions and ways to help answer then.

Why didn't God create good people?

He did! Genesis 1:27 says, "God created man in his own image, in the image of God he created him; male and female he created them." How much better can we ask for? God loves us so much He also gave us the ability and privilege to make choices. What we do with those choices is up to us individually. Those who choose to be close to God will reject those things that are not of God: all that is evil. I'm glad I can choose to love the Lord and follow Him. He loves us enough to let us make the choice. People are bad, evil, or wicked because they choose to be, not because God made them that way. But God did provide a way to save us all in spite of our sin nature. He sent Jesus to be our Savior; He leaves the choice to us.

Wouldn't it have been better if God had never created people? Obviously God didn't think so. When we are suffering it would seem better to never have been born. In Job

3:3 Job says, "May the day of my birth perish, and the night it was said, 'A boy is born!'" Even a man of God like Job thought it better to never have been born because of how he was suffering. But God's plan and wisdom are much bigger than we can even begin to fathom. Fortunately He included a plan of redemption and salvation and a way to deliver us from potential suffering; we need but ask Him to give us peace.

Why doesn't God eliminate all the evil people in the world?

Is it safe to say we are all sinners? Yes it is. Roman's 3:23 says, "for ALL have sinned and fall short of the glory of God." (Emphasis added) In fact we're all dead in sin. Roman's 6:23 says, "For the wages of sin is death." If we stopped right there, things would look pretty bleak for our spiritual future. However, that same verse goes on to say, "but the FREE GIFT of God is eternal life in Christ Jesus our Lord." (Emphasis added) If God eliminated all the evil people of the world, none of us would be left. In God's eyes, sin is sin! So when it comes to lying, stealing, committing adultery, or murder, they are all the same in God's eyes. Why did God give us the Ten Commandments? It was a guide to instruct us in the way we should live. But more so, to illustrate how much we need Him in our lives and how much we need the forgiveness provided us by Jesus death on the cross. Think about it, we can hardly get through a day without breaking one of them. If you ever told a lie or lusted in your heart you have sinned.

Why doesn't an all-powerful God intercede and deal with all the consequences of evil in the world?

He did by sending His son to die for our sins. The ultimate consequence of evil in the world is spending eternity

QUESTIONS OR EXCUSES   **121**

separated from the presence of the Father. If God stepped in and stopped all the consequences of evil people at the time it was happening, the world, as we know it would stop. And many times we are suffering from the results of our own actions. To stop all the consequences of evil would mean stopping the human race.

Why doesn't God stop this specific suffering in my life?

Dealing with difficulty is not all bad. Suffering builds character. It is when we are dealing with difficult circumstances that we find out what we're made of. We know Jesus was God in the flesh, but many of us sometimes forget that Jesus was also a man, a human, feeling and dealing with the same emotions and temptations we must face everyday of our lives. But instead of acting on His own selfish needs, He did what God wanted and instructed Him to do. He followed God's will, not his own. There is no better illustration of this in the Bible than when Jesus prayed at Gethsemane the night of his arrest. In Matthew 26:39, Jesus prays, "My Father, if it is possible, let this cup pass from me; yet not as I will, but as Thou wilt." He knew what was in store for Him, but He said, "your will Father, not mine." He knew He was part of a plan that only God knew. If God had spared Him the pain and suffering of the cross, where would we be now? The consequences cannot be put into words!

Many times when we are tempted, we only think of the short-term pleasure, or, as in Jesus' case, the avoidance of additional pain in our lives. The easy way out: Our way. Then we get mad at God when we suffer the consequences of our impulsiveness and selfishness. We not only blame God, we blame everyone except ourselves. We make excuses, but when it comes right down to the heart of the matter, it's our own heart we must look at. Are we really trying to follow

God's will and live according to His plan or are we simply pretending?

How much easier would God's job be if we asked to know His will before, instead of after, we made a choice? But even after we get in over our heads, after we've got things as messed up as humanly possible, He is always there to bail us out of whatever we've got ourselves into. We need but ask... It doesn't matter what the circumstances are. "And we know that in ALL things God works for the good of those who love Him, who have been called according to His purpose" (Emphasis added) (Romans 8:28). Jesus didn't have to suffer for us; He chose to! If He didn't die willingly, there would have been no point in dying at all. He had to want to do God's will. God wasn't going to force Him to do His will, what a sacrifice! He could have said no, asked what's the use and chalked us up as lost causes. Praise Jesus; He didn't.

Jesus set the example for us all. If we serve the Lord for any reason other than loving the Lord and wanting to serve him, we're wasting our time; it's nothing but empty gestures: we're pretending. Do you think Satan tempted Him: you can bet he did! The Bible is full of examples of temptations we all face and the result of giving into them. David let temptation get the best of him. A man, the Bible describes as, a man after God's own heart, and he suffered. But everyone, regardless of his or her sin, can be forgiven. What a wonderful source of hope! The thief on the cross next to Jesus is a perfect example of the hope we have in Jesus. He didn't confess his sins to Jesus, he didn't say a sinner's prayer, and he wasn't baptized, he simply said, "Jesus, remember me when you come into your kingdom" (Luke 23:42). And Jesus replied, "I tell you the truth, today you will be with me in paradise" (Luke 23:43).

On the cross, right before he died, the thief acknowledges Jesus as Lord with this simple statement of faith and immediately he receives forgiveness and Jesus promises him a home in heaven! We all have this gift available to us if we follow that thief's example and acknowledge that Jesus is Lord and the only way to heaven. Why does God allow us to suffer? Suffering builds character: Christian character.

14 DECEPTION

What a term, "New Age" everybody has a better answer to life's toughest questions, yet when everything is said and done, people find themselves at the cross of Christ. How many times did the Israelites turn away from God to worship idols only to return to God when their "New Age" gods didn't produce? Nothing has changed in thousands of years. Human selfishness and lusts of the flesh send people on a search for gods or spirituality that allows them to do as they wish and still claim to be a spiritual or religious person. But their conscience will not permit them to rest. They know in their hearts that their actions are wrong, because of the innate knowledge of God that every human possesses. This is the very thing Freud struggled with throughout his life. His God was himself.

When people think this way they are playing right into Satan's hands. He wants them to reject Jesus for a spirituality that leads them to hell. We see the effect of this New Age thinking in the church today. Many established denominations are compromising the principles the Bible teaches. Some examples are performing homosexual weddings and allowing homosexuals to be members of the clergy even though God's word tells us, in the book of Romans, as well as many other versus, that homosexuality is an abomination to God.

These are not my words but God's. As I said earlier,

believing the Bible is an all or nothing process, we can't believe that God got part of His word right but goofed up other parts. If that's the case then what are we to believe? Is the part that tells us how to receive forgiveness right? What about all the history in the Bible that archeology and science continue to validate year after year? Or the existence of the patriarchs, if Abraham never existed, then Christianity, Judaism, and the Muslim faiths are all based on a fictitious character. If I don't believe in the whole of God's word, then my faith is meaningless. There is overwhelming evidence historically, scientifically, but most important spiritually that the Bible is indeed the truth.

The Episcopal Church is on the verge of a split due to the confirmation of an openly gay Bishop. If some members of the Episcopal Church feel the portion of scripture referring to homosexuality is irrelevant, then what other parts of scripture are open for compromise? Does this mean we shouldn't love homosexuals as Christ loves us? I think not, but the church shouldn't condone homosexuality by performing homosexual marriages or permitting homosexuals to preach the word of God either. Many non-Christians know what the Bible says about homosexuality, what kind of a message does this send to non-believers and believers that are babes in Christ? These mixed messages lead people astray or keep them from searching out the truth about God.

Another example of deception are the many programs that attempt to help those struggling with addiction problems that speak of strength from an unnamed higher power. If Satan can de-Christianize the church, he should have no trouble with organizations that talk of a higher power without speaking of a specific deity. Many people entering recovery programs are searching for answers and are very vulnerable to false teachings. The door is open to any pop psychologist and their psychobabble to negatively influence people during times of vulnerability. This is very evident in any bookstores self-help section. What's ironic though is that the Bible continues to be the best selling book in the world.

An example of New Age thinking can be found in a book by M. Scott Peck called, *The Road Less Traveled*. The front cover says, "A new psychology of love, traditional values, and spiritual growth." In a section titled "The Religion of Science," he tells his readers, "The path to holiness lies through questioning everything. We begin by replacing the religion of our parents with the religion of science. We must rebel against and reject the religion of our parents, for inevitably their world view will be narrower than that of which we are capable if we take full advantage of our personal experience, including our adult experience and the experience of an additional generation of human history. So for mental health and spiritual growth we must develop our own religion and not rely on that of our parents."[1]

I agree with the premise that we must challenge religious paradigms, to exclude useless religiosity while being careful not to exclude Jesus. As I mentioned earlier, religion turns many people away from Jesus, but developing new religions isn't the answer, developing a relationship with Christ is. But that's exactly what continues to happen now, as it did thousands of years ago, people are creating their own religions and in the process turning people away from the true and living God. And where is this way of thinking leading us? Everywhere you look, the disintegration of values is obvious. Is this the wider worldview Peck speaks of?

Some people commit their lives to bringing the truth of Christ to others, while false teachers promote their own brand of religion. Andre Kole is a person dedicated to bringing the truth to others. He is a highly respected Christian illusionist. He is a world-class performer consulting with the likes of David Copperfield, Siegfried and Roy and Harry Blackstone, because of his expertise in creating illusions. This may be troubling to some Christians unless they know something about his mission in life.

He travels around the world teaching the gospel of Christ to others by performing illusions. He has spent much of his life exposing the charlatans that claim to perform miracles through spirituality and supernatural powers. He defines a magician as one who uses natural means to accomplish a supernatural effect (Kole, 1998).[2]

He not only presents the gospel in a very entertaining fashion but he challenges anyone claiming to have supernatural powers to prove it to him without using the tricks of the trade. For example, he offers anyone that can levitate without props one thousand dollars a second for up to 25 seconds. He says that in thirty years he has never had a taker. He demonstrates many of the tricks so called psychics and spiritualist do, including psychic surgery, to dupe people out of their money. He says they are frauds. He also says that any eight-year-old child can do what he does with 25 years of practice.

Unfortunately, the church contributes to this spiritual confusion. Religious tradition and ritual turns many people away from God every day. Not the teachings of scripture mind you, but the religiosity of man: the man-made do's and don'ts. If we are truly following the Lord and trying to win others to Christ we must let Him do the convicting and judging, not us.

We must preach and counsel according to God's word, not ours, in order to plant the seeds that He grows. We are held accountable for how we represent God through our lives and His word. May we let His Spirit speak to others and not our interpretation of what He's trying to say? In this way, we will not be false teachers of God's word. We must present the gospel just as God gives it to us. This way people can make a choice to accept or reject Jesus. Their choice depends on accurate information. Once they know and understand the Truth, it's their choice...

Choices

Why me? This is a question so many ask when they find themselves in the mist of a difficult situation. I have made many poor choices in my life. As I said earlier, the Lord tried to keep me on the right path even when I wasn't seeking His advice. But being the loving and gracious God He is, He allowed me to choose what path to take. I truly believe He kept a hedge around me to protect me against myself, but not to the point that I wouldn't have to deal with the consequences of my decisions.

I also asked, why me? Like I was an innocent victim of circumstances beyond my control, when I had nobody to blame but myself. So many times I made choices I thought were best and left the Lord completely out of the loop. Then I would find myself in a compromising or uncomfortable situation and ask the Lord how He could allow this to happen to me when I didn't ask for His opinion to begin with. He didn't get me into the mess, I did! Then I would plead with Him to help me out. What's most amazing is that He did. It might not be the way I would choose but He was always there and, in the long run, it always turned out better than I imagined.

When I started including God in my decision making process, my decisions got much better. Sometimes we do fall victim to things beyond our control. But how much control do we really have to begin with? Control is a ruse of the devil. We really have no control over anything including ourselves, that's why we need God so much. We can influence our children, friends and co-workers but we can't stop them from doing something if they're mind is set on doing it. If we could control ourselves, we wouldn't do things that we know are going to get us in trouble. Control is an illusion.

When we do find ourselves in difficult circumstances that we have no control over, we can think of Job. God acknowledged that he was a righteous man and he still suffered more than most of us can even imagine. Jesus was sinless, but look at what happened to Him. The Bible tells us in several passages that the Lord uses trials to mold us in His image. Job says this in the midst of his suffering, he says, "But he knows the way that I take; when he has tested me, I will come forth as gold" (Job 23:10). If Jesus suffered as He did and He was blameless, I think it would be very arrogant to think we shouldn't suffer. Instead of asking why me, ask why not me?

So does loving the Lord and doing His will mean suffering? Sometimes it does. Things will still not always go the way we think they should and the unexpected still happens; many times it's painful. The difference is how we cope with those things. Now we have the strength of God to sustain us. And suffering is what not only draws us closer to Jesus, but it's also what makes us more like Jesus. Christian means Christ-like. Isn't that what we're suppose to be striving for? Regardless of the circumstances, suffering people must trust the Lord. Choose wisely. . .

15 SOME OF SATAN'S FAVORITE TACTICS

Satan is the father of lies and the master of deception. "For there is no truth in him. When he lies, he speaks his native language, for he is a liar and the father of lies" (John 8:44). He's an accuser, and the Bible says he (the devil) prowls around like a lion waiting to attack (1 Peter 5:8). He thrives on and exploits are weaknesses. That's why Paul tells us we should dress ourselves in the full armor of God. "Therefore put on the full armor of God, so that when the day of evil comes, you may be able to stand your ground, and after you have done everything, to stand. Stand firm then, with the belt of truth buckled around your waist, with the breastplate of righteousness in place, and with your feet fitted with the readiness that comes from the gospel of peace. In addition to all this, take up the shield of faith, with which you can extinguish all the flaming arrows of the evil one. Take the helmet of salvation and the sword of the Spirit, which is the word of God" (Ephesians 6:13-17). When he finds a chink in our armor, he attacks. He ravages our society by invading our homes and our churches.

He uses sex, drug abuse, especially alcohol, conflict, and divorce to destroy our communities, families, and lives. I mention these specific areas for two reasons. The first reason is their prevalence in our society. They're everywhere you look: television programming, advertising, movies, and sporting events are all venues for one or more of these issues. Soap Operas count on all of these vices to draw an audience. Movies are inundated with sexually explicit material, and alcohol is a favorite at sporting events.

The second reason is the reluctance of the church to deal with these issues. They are difficult issues to deal with but they are the major contributors to the disintegration of our society and families. People should be getting guidance from their church family about these issues but they're reluctant to discuss these types of problems with anyone involved with the church because of the stigma, perception, and/or reality that these subjects are taboo in a church setting or they might be looked at as weak if they are struggling in one or more of these areas.

Churches are becoming more willing to address these issues. I listen to Charles Swindoll and Charles Stanley's radio programs on a regular basis. Many times I've heard them address these issues on their programs blending frankness with compassion. This type of leadership will go a long way in encouraging church members, dealing with difficult issues, to turn to their church leaders and church family, instead of secular counselors, in their time of need. It is no accident that these issues, that are so prevalent in the destruction of our society, are issues that cause discomfort in the church.

If the church steers away from these issues, Satan has free rein to do as he pleases without a system of checks and balances. The church is the moral fabric of our society, which is all the more reason that churches must teach and practice the truth about Jesus, drawing people to Christ, not practicing religion or hypocrisy and pushing them away. They must also step up to deal with the problems that continue to destroy our society. The next section deals with these issues.

To Drink or Not to Drink

For years I've heard people in church say Christians shouldn't drink alcohol because the Bible says we shouldn't. I have found nothing in the scriptures that directs us to abstain from consuming fermented drink. I've heard people say that when the Bible mentions wine, it means grape juice, but several of the references I found speak specifically of fermented drink. Here is an example, "You ate no bread and drank no wine or other fermented drink. I did this so that you might know that I am the LORD your God" (Deuteronomy 29:6).

A person that enjoys an occasional beer or glass of wine is not a sinner condemned to hell. The problem is that many people can't enjoy an occasional drink without allowing their behavior to get out of control. Although the Bible doesn't forbid the use of fermented drink, it does warn of the consequences of abusing alcohol. I would agree; however, that the best way to avoid abusing alcohol is to never use it. This is a subject of continual debate and if a person has a problem with behavior when consuming alcohol they should simply stay away from it.

This is one of the areas that the church could do a much better job in educating and assisting people. When a person is dealing with any kind of substance abuse it's a part of their life they are not proud of and usually try to keep to themselves. This only exacerbates the problem, even if they are trying to quit, because they are going it alone. They need to know that there are people that care about them and a God that loves them and can help if they ask. Alcoholics Anonymous (A.A.) is a very successful organization that helps people fight addiction. They teach members to draw on the strength of a power greater than their own. If we're doing our job in the church, we can introduce them to that greater power so they can have a personal relationship with Him.

It's not just the person struggling with the abuse or addiction problem that needs help. Family members need just as much attention. The dysfunction created by substance abuse is very damaging to the entire family. It can make it very difficult for a person growing up in that environment to allow themselves to trust the Lord because exposure to that environment makes trusting anyone, including God, extremely difficult. Plenty of love and support can help teach people to trust, but it takes time and patience. What follows are just some of the issues victims of substance abuse must cope with.

Spiritual Life of Adult Children of Alcoholics

If there is a God, how could he let this happen to my family and me, does he care, if so, why not does He do something, why isn't He listening, can't He hear my prayers? I'm very familiar with these questions. Alcoholism has been a part of my life since I can remember. Many people, especially in today's society, grow up with fathers that are poor examples to follow. So it stands to reason that if God the Father is anything like many earthly fathers, how can they expect much from Him either? The best example I had of what God expected from a father while I was growing up was my grandfather. He worked hard, was an honest businessman, and always found time for his family. He also loved unconditionally and was always very generous to others. It is his influence that brought me to know Christ.

People fear what they do not understand. An alcoholic is a very difficult person to understand. Many people have very little understanding of God, when you put these two facts together it is no wonder why a child growing up in an alcoholic home would fear God. First they have a distorted image of God to begin with. When added to the element of the unknown, God or the idea of God becomes a frightening thought.

Alcoholic parents are physically away from their children much of the time. When they are physically present in the home, they remain emotionally absent. Cecil G. Osborne says, "An absentee father can mean an absentee God."[1] If a child's only reference to a heavenly Father is their earthly father this seems very logical. They attribute the characteristics they see in their earthly fathers to God. They see God as cold, distant, indifferent, unloving, and powerless to act on a person's behalf. Because alcoholics are unapproachable, an adult child my think the same of God.

Is God weak and powerless, is He a being that I should pity instead of worship, is He an angry judgmental God? These are valid questions considering the type of a father or mother an adult child of alcoholics grew up with. Children of alcoholics do whatever they can to please the alcoholic parent. They want to be looked on favorably. They want to please the parent and make them as happy as possible. If I try just a little harder to be a good kid they'll be proud of me and be happy. So it is in their relationship with God. Believers in recovery, for addiction or dysfunction, may deem it necessary to earn God's favor, if I try a little harder God will approve of me. In essence, they are trying to work their way to heaven instead of relying on God's grace through Jesus Christ.

Closely related to this misperception is that God demands perfection from His followers. Alcoholics are very critical of those around them. They are impulsive and impatient. Children of alcoholics tend to be perfectionists and think God expects them to be perfect. God knows how far we are from perfect that's why He sent His Son to die for us. Control is always an issue in an alcoholic home too. Many people growing up in healthy environments reject following God because they feel that they will have to give up so much. How much more difficult is choosing God for a child that never enjoyed freedom in their actions. Believing they have options while following Christ is hard to believe.

Forgiveness is another area of difficulty for adult children of alcoholics. It is virtually nonexistent in an alcoholic home. The alcoholic doesn't extend forgiveness to a child that makes a mistake, which reinforces the message, be perfect or I reject you. This leaves the child wondering how can God forgive me? Adult children also have trouble forgiving themselves. They tend to be judgmental of themselves and others.

Judgmental Christians are poor witnesses for Christ because nobody wants to be around them or the God they profess. Therefore, their spiritual lives are usually void of the joy experienced in serving the Lord and leading others to Christ. This is one reason adult children find it difficult to develop a close relationship with God. Another reason is that they find it difficult to have a close relationship with an unseen God when they can't have a relationship with humans they see everyday.

The importance of trust in any relationship cannot be overstated. Without trust there is no relationship; this includes a relationship with Jesus. Adult children already know they can't trust their parents. And how can they trust a God that would allow this kind of pain and suffering to happen to them? They must understand that they are blaming God for their pain and suffering the same way their parents blame them for their alcoholism. So how does a person's trust develop and grow in a relationship with God and

SOME OF SATAN'S FAVORITE TACTICS 139

how do they know it's God's voice they hear when making a decision; the way it does in any relationship: by spending time with the other person. The Bible tells us to seek and we will find (God).

I struggled with the question of a loving God allowing bad things to happen to good people, especially innocent children. Reading God's word gave me some insight into this disturbing question but I also researched other sources for information. Lee Strobel, interviewed Peter Kreeft, Ph.D. on the subject of how evil and suffering can exist along with a loving and compassionate God. During the interview, Strobel restated a response Kreeft gave to a question. Strobel said, "Then God created evil." Kreeft replied, "No, he created the possibility of evil; people actualized that potentiality. The source of evil is not God's power but mankind's freedom."[2] God loves us so much, He gives us the freedom to accept or reject Him. If we were incapable of choosing, we'd be nothing more than robots. It's our freedom to choose that enables evil to exist. Christians can help adult children begin to break down the barriers to faith in Christ by helping them understand that people are evil not God.

They also need to understand that God wants the best for them and their family but He can't help them until they trust Him. This doesn't mean a superficial trust but a complete trust: with all of their heart. "Trust in the Lord with all of your heart and lean not on your own understanding; in all your ways acknowledge Him and He will make your paths straight" (Proverbs 3:5-6). Sometimes we can't understand the Lord's ways, but as we pray and read His word we come to have a greater understanding of Him. We can never completely understand Him because He is God and we are not; that's where faith begins and where understanding ends. We build trust in relationships through communication and the passage of time. Trust doesn't happen over night; however, it can be lost in an instant.

Satan wants to prevent us from having a personal relationship with Christ and he will do anything to keep it from happening. New Christians or those struggling with their faith are prime targets for attack. I Peter 5:8 says Christians, "Be sober, be vigilant; because your adversary the devil, prowls around like a roaring lion looking for someone to devour." He can't take away their salvation but he can discourage and frustrate them to the point that they are not effective witnesses for Christ. Pastors, counselors, and others providing support in these situations face quite a dilemma here.

Many Christians, more so, those that are new or struggling with their faith, have a difficult time comprehending Satan's power and really don't want to talk about it. It is frightening. But they need to know it's real and he is the enemy not God. He uses our weaknesses to control us. In the alcoholic's case, it's the alcohol. Dr. Rebecca Brown calls our vulnerabilities doorways for Satan. He is formidable and humans are powerless to fight against him on their own. She goes on to say, "We can stand against and overcome Satan only with the power of Jesus Christ."[3] Satan likes it when we're down and that's where he wants to keep us. Encouragement to persevere is a very effective tool for those providing support.

It's extremely important to reinforce, to those in recovery, that God loves them and wants to have a personal relationship with them. He is a God that is trustworthy and dependable and He is willing to help anyone who asks, but it goes back to choices. If an alcoholic chooses to continue to drink, he or she will continue to suffer the consequences of that choice. Adult children also have a choice, to continue living in denial and rejecting God or accepting the truth about their family and asking God to grant them peace and teach them to forgive.

If alcoholics practiced empathy, they probably wouldn't be alcoholics. If they were capable of putting themselves in their family member's shoes, they would realize how much they are hurting them and how much emotional damage they are causing to everyone around them. A little understanding goes a long way especially where forgiveness is concerned. When a person tries to look at a situation from another's perspective, they begin to break down barriers and open the door for forgiveness to take place.

The irony is that the children are the innocent people in an alcoholic home and they are the ones seeking forgiveness. They feel guilty for the parent's alcoholism because of the parent constantly shifting blame to the other family members. But without God, Satan will continue to wreak havoc in the lives of everyone involved. Alcoholics and adult children of alcoholics need the assurance that although the road to recovery may be long and demanding, it is worth the journey. For at the end, if they trust God, they will learn to love, trust and forgive. They will also have a peace that surpasses understanding and learn to function in a healthy way.

Marriage and Divorce

How is marriage a problem for the church, isn't the church the institution in our society that encourages and performs marriages? Two problems immediately come to mind. First, some churches refuse to marry couples if either person is divorced or if couples are living together. Divorce should not be a reason to refuse marrying a couple. Without knowing the circumstances of the divorce, it is a judgmental attitude that refuses to perform a marriage.

If a couple is living together and want to marry, it is quite possible that convictions about living together are driving their decision. To refuse to marry them is contributing to the sin they are trying to do something about. What's worse is the church that refuses to allow a couple to join because they're living together. If they want to join, they will probably want to attend, which allows them to hear God's word and convict them to change their living arrangements. If living in sin is the issue, then none of us should be in church because of our sin, but isn't that precisely why we're there in the first place. All have sinned; some are just more obvious and honest about their sin than others.

We don't have to condone their behavior or be judgmental of them; we must instruct them in the way of the Lord leaving our own convictions out of it. Helping them understand God's instruction will be more beneficial in correcting their path than harsh admonishment. This is the second area where the church can make a huge difference: providing premarital counseling.

Divorce and cohabitation are not ideal situations for sure, but they are a fact of life. Many people live together because of their fear of divorce. Whether they've been party to divorce as children or as an adult, they know how painful divorce can be. They don't like being alone but they don't like being hurt either. People often rush into marriage for all the wrong reasons and then find themselves in a situation they were ill prepared for. Pastors can provide an invaluable service to couples considering marriage by insisting that the couple receive premarital counseling before they perform a marriage. By doing so, it helps the couple fully understand what they are committing to, regardless if this is a first or subsequent marriage.

SOME OF SATAN'S FAVORITE TACTICS

We live in a throwaway society that views commitment with disdain. The prevailing attitude seems to be, "I'm here until I find something better." Like I said, people rush into marriage for all the wrong reasons; to get out of the house, for financial stability, because of unplanned pregnancies, and so on. They have little, if any, understanding of what commitment is, especially if they are from a broken or dysfunctional home. Premarital counseling can go a long way in helping couples consider issues they may otherwise overlook without the guidance that a pastor or other church leaders can provide.

Premarital counseling can help couples understand that marriage is a life-long commitment. It can also help them understand the meaning of love. Many people confuse love and lust. This leads them to believe that love is a feeling. Love is a commitment. We chose to spend the rest of our lives with our spouse after getting to know them. It's not an instantaneous decision we make on our first date. We learn to love our mates over a period of time. There are always times of disagreement but that shouldn't be the norm.

Couples need to understand that not only are the dynamics of their relationship in a constant state of change, but all of their relationships are constantly changing. When we get upset with our children, we don't stop loving them, so why do we do that with spouses. How do you fall in and out of love? It's more accurate to say we fall in and out of commitment. You're not what I want anymore so I'm moving on. . . to what? If we learned to love a person in the first place, why can't we do it again? It takes effort and time, but it's worth it.

Over time, the physical passion in a relationship gives way to a more mature expression of love where communication is key to the success of the marriage. That doesn't mean the passion isn't there anymore, it just changes. People think that when the passion subsides, the relationship is over. They feel it is necessary to search out a partner that will rekindle the passion they once felt for their spouse. What they fail to realize is, like everything else that becomes familiar to us, we must continue to reinvent our relationships to keep them from becoming stagnant. People only look at immediate satisfaction instead of long-term consequences.

The grass is always greener on the other side of the fence, but that's because someone else is caring for that grass. If we end up taking care of that lawn and don't change how we care for it, when the seasons change, we will have a mess on our hands. The same is true with our relationships. If we continue relating to our spouse without considering the ever-changing dynamics of our relationship, we will have a real mess to deal with. Sometimes those messes become unmanageable. When this happens, couples look for a way out and that often leads to divorce.

Divorce

Divorce is an issue, that traditionally, many churches have trouble dealing with. My experience suggests that there are certain issues that church staffs are either not well trained to deal with or they're very uncomfortable dealing with and that is the subject of this next section. I've heard church leaders say that seminary does a great job of preparing them to teach others about the Bible but is less effective in training pastors to be effective counselors. One area that seems to be a major area of concern is divorce.

Divorced people can face much trepidation depending on the stance of the church. Some churches will not allow divorced people to join and if they do, they will not allow them to hold leadership positions in the church. Some

SOME OF SATAN'S FAVORITE TACTICS

145

pastors refuse to perform marriages in the church if either person getting married is previously divorced. And in some cases, divorced people just feel uncomfortable because of the attitudes of the church members regarding their divorce. I do see a change for the positive in this area but there is still much room for improvement.

Divorce is an ugly situation no matter how agreeable the couple divorcing is to one another, especially when kids are involved. The church should be a source of support through a difficult situation like divorce not an added source of aggravation. Many times the aggravation is due to what I talked about earlier: religious interpretation. The Bible is very clear about the Lord's opinion of divorce in both the Old and New Testaments. Nobody in the church should advocate or sanction divorce, but when it happens, they should not be judgmental either.

I stated earlier that I'm divorced. I did not want to divorce, and feel I did everything possible to avoid it, but when it happened, those I went to church with did not subject me to more grief. In fact, it was quite the opposite. My brothers and sisters in Christ rallied around me and provided me with incredible support. I was fortunate that I went to a church where I received so much support, but that's not always the case.

In some of the churches that I've attended, church members, including the leadership, made those that were divorced or going through divorce feel uncomfortable and sometimes unwelcome in the church. Some people living with an abusive spouse will stay in an abusive relationship for fear of excommunication because of the churches stance on divorce. Is this right?

As I said earlier, we live in a throwaway society where it is acceptable to get rid of something when it no longer satisfies us. People are always looking for an easy solution to the problems they face and divorce has become a quick fix or so people think. They only look at the short-term outcome and overlook the long-term consequences. They fail to see two very important factors that will have a continuing impact on their life.

The first factor is they seem to forget that even though they are divorced from the apparent source of their aggravation, they still have to deal with that person on a regular basis if they have children between them. The second is, they may have been the majority of the problem in the relationship and will be in subsequent relationships. They are dysfunctional and will seek out someone that will allow them to continue interacting in a way they are familiar with, someone that behaves much the same way their previous spouse did. This perpetuates the dysfunction and eventually they watch their subsequent relationship(s) suffer the same demise.

Most of the time church leaders and laypeople in the church do not know all the dynamics of a troubled relationship, and even if they are close to one or both parties involved in the relationship they are usually getting only one side of the story. Getting involved and taking sides or giving advice, particularly advice based on personal opinion and not on scripture, can make the situation worse, but remaining neutral and supportive can be very beneficial and possibly help lead to reconciliation. That's why it's imperative for church members and leaders to be more cognizant of their reactions to those dealing with divorce.

What Believers Can Do to Keep Those Dealing with Divorce from Turning Away From the Church?

Unfortunately I had to deal with this issue personally

both as a child of divorced parents and as an adult. I had no support system as a child, which made a difficult situation even worse. As an adult, I was determined that my children would never have to suffer through the same thing I did as a child, but despite my best effort, they did. Although it was extremely difficult, I was able to endure a great deal more than I thought myself capable because of the ongoing love and support of believers around me; more so than even my own family gave me. As an instructor and counselor, many express to me their discontent with churches when dealing with relationship issues including divorce. The tendency to be judgmental of others will surely turn them away; as is the case with many people that I speak to.

I fell away from God a few years into my marriage and that was the beginning of the end of my marriage. We weren't attending church and because I was a psychology student, I thought I could figure everything out myself. Things continued to deteriorate to the point that reconciliation seemed impossible and in the end it was. After I moved out, feeling I'd lost everything and very angry about the circumstances surrounding our separation, I found myself at the doorstep of a church talking to a preacher I didn't know. God led me to this place and this person just when I needed to be there most. My life has never been the same.

This man and the people of the church supported me in a way I didn't think possible. They encouraged me to stay in my marriage and did not condemn either of us for actions that exacerbated the situation. For five years we prayed together, laughed together, and cried together. To that point, nothing in regard to my marriage changed but God was doing awesome things in my heart. Once I realized that divorce was inevitable, I asked my preacher for the name of a Christian attorney.

I mentioned earlier that I wanted someone that valued the sanctity of marriage and not someone who took great joy at getting as much as they could regardless of the cost to the family. This was to be a critical factor in the outcome. My attorney did everything in his power to encourage my wife to rethink her position about our marriage but to no avail. The divorce proceeded in a very peaceful fashion and to this day I have a very good relationship with the mother of my two oldest children. How does this answer the question of how believers can keep a person from turning away from the church at such a critical time in their life? God answers the question with this statement, "love thy neighbor." Everyone involved continued to love my family and me and allowed God to deal with the rest. As believers, we must admonish with biblical guidance and continue to love and let the Lord take care of the rest.

We should do everything we can to encourage couples to stay together but when they don't, we need not excommunicate them. If others are living life styles we don't condone we shouldn't push them out of the church or make them feel unwanted. We must teach them what God's word says, not what our interpretation is, and let the Holy Spirit speak to their hearts. And He will. Regardless if a person or family is pre, during, or post divorce, they need our love and understanding, not our criticism.

16 SEX AND THE CHURCH

Sex was, and in some ways still is, something people, especially "good Christians" don't talk about. Until the advent of Acquired Immune Deficiency Syndrome (AIDS), discussions about sex were left to locker rooms or other similar venues. Who could even imagine talking to their pastor about sexual issues and/or other related problems? Ignorance about sex is a major cause of the transmission of sexual diseases and unplanned pregnancies. Many churches are quick to condemn abortions but seem very reluctant to help prevent them.

Sexual counseling is also an important part of premarital counseling. Because people confuse love with lust, this counseling can help preclude marital problems due to this confusion and help keep lines of communication open to resolve difficulties when they arise. Couples need to know that sex is a gift from God and that He wants us to enjoy our sexual relationship with our spouse. Many people raised in a religious environment receive misinformation about sex and consequently this can lead to problems in an otherwise healthy relationship.

Pastors or trained staff counselors can do a great service to the congregation and the community by providing counseling about sexual issues. After AIDS became an epidemic, people were more willing to discuss sex openly but most of the focus was on preventing the spread of AIDS and not on the ramifications of premarital sex or sexual

Inappropriate Sexual Behavior

dysfunction in marriage, which can lead to relationship problems. By offering couples a place to go and discuss these issues, the church can play an integral role in holding a marriage together. The next section discusses some of these issues.

Inappropriate Sexual Behavior

Why should sexual behavior be a concern for the church? In days past, the church would likely be the last place someone would go to get help for inappropriate sexual behavior and the same is probably true today. There is an incredible stigma attached to dealing with issues of sexuality. But the denial of human sexuality and the power it wields over some, no doubt contributed to the crisis in the Catholic Church. Church leaders are more likely to deal with the sexual ills of our society in more public ways. For example, religious groups continually fight to keep pornography in check, but to no avail. Now it is more available than ever to anyone on the Internet. What's worse is people don't have to worry about getting caught buying it at a local convenience store. It is available in the privacy of their home.

It's bad enough that the temptation to look at it is in many stores that we frequent everyday. Any video store can accommodate anyone looking for lots of explicate sex; and, anyone can maintain anonymity by subscribing to their magazine of choice. I've struggled with this problem myself. I still have to be vigilant and, at times, ask God for strength when I feel tempted. It gets easier to resist as my faith grows. The Bible says "resist the devil and he will flee from you" (James 4:7). Satan's a bully and bullies search out easy targets. When you stand up to him (resist) with the help of the Holy Spirit, he'll eventually leave you alone to search out easier prey, but don't let your guard down because he'll attack if he sees an opportunity.

Sometimes I felt like I was the only person that aspires to serve God in a full-time ministry that had a problem controlling my desire to sneak a peak at a beautiful woman, but recently I was listening to Charles Swindoll's radio program and he revealed some very startling statistics. Speaking about accountability, he specifically mentioned Internet pornography. He said over 50 percent of the men attending a large spiritual gathering viewed a pornographic web-sight less than seven days before attending the conference and that 50 percent of pastors responding to a survey admitted viewing pornography in the past 12 months.

This is not an indictment against pastors. Pastors are tempted like everyone else. It's an effort to point out the difficulty people have when temptation is readily available and the necessity for the church to pay more attention to human sexuality instead of pretending it's not a problem for "good Christians." There are many good people struggling and they need to know they have a place to go to help them deal with their struggle. The Catholic Church ignored human sexuality for many years and look what happened.

Principles Regarding Roles of Sexuality From the Old and New Testaments

The Old Testament's description of human sexuality "they will become one flesh" (Genesis 2:24), is a concept many people, including many Christians, do not completely understand. I believe most people understand this to be a sexual union: physical-to-physical, flesh-to-flesh. The emotional and spiritual dimensions, especially the spiritual dimension, are an afterthought if they're even thought about at all. What is lost is the true beauty of the human sexual experience the way God intended it to be: a truly fulfilling experience, physically, emotionally, and spiritually! Sex for simple physical gratification is simply a meaningless act of lust!

When all the aspects of human sexuality, the physical, emotional, and spiritual come to bear in a relationship, the relationship is fulfilling and lasting. God made us to be sexual in nature, however; when sex is simply for physical reward, the essence God intended for sex in human relationships is minimized or completely lost. Consequently, relationships suffer. When we allow our sexuality to drive us to sin, our relationship with our spouse is not the only one to suffer; our relationship with God also suffers.

Much of what we learn in the Old Testament concerning sexuality had to do with Old Testament law structured in terms of property rights, sanitation, and behavior. Living conditions, and social and religious rituals must be understood to keep the teachings of the Old Testament from being taken out of context. Women were considered as property and considered an asset if they satisfied their husband's needs, including sex. Men and women did not live by the same sexual standards, but nowhere, in the Old Testament does God condone sexual misconduct, by a man or woman.

The teaching of the New Testament is a radical departure from that of the Old Testament in that the New Testament teaches mutuality. It teaches that men and women have equal rights to sexual pleasure and release. The sexual standards for men and women are the same. This is due to Christ breaking down the barriers between men and women. Galatians 3:28 says, "There is neither Jew nor Greek, slave nor free, male nor female, for all are one in Jesus Christ." This puts us all on equal ground. Christ broke down all the human barriers.

Although Christ broke down all these barriers by dying on the cross, we do our very best to construct new ones. Society and religion are notorious for creating ludicrous standards in the name of the Bible. Unfortunately, many unhealthy sexual paradigms still exist creating problems in marital relationships. These can lead to an unhealthy sexual relationship in the marriage, which leads to other problems in the relationship that slowly erode the marriage.

The New Testament does not create these barriers. It clearly states that sex is not just all right in God's eyes, but it's a blessing, a gift from God for us to enjoy with our spouses! The Bible says, "Do not deprive each other..." Love, not lust, should be the guiding principle for our sexual behavior in marriage" (1 Corinthians 7:3). The Bible does not put any limitations on how to enjoy sex within marriage. In fact, The Song of Solomon, in the Old Testament, is one of the most sensuous pieces of literature ever written and it's part of the Bible! Inspired by God!

To put our marital relationships in perspective, the Bible compares our love for our spouse in terms of Christ's love for the church, incredible! "Husbands, love your wives, just as Christ loved the church and gave himself up for her... husbands ought to love their wives as their own bodies. He who loves his wife loves himself" (Ephesians 5:25,28). The Song of Solomon beautifully illustrates the passion we should expect to experience if we follow the biblical standards concerning our sexuality. Becoming one flesh means uniting two personalities, physically, emotionally, and spiritually.

God intends for us to enjoy our sexuality with our spouse. He made us to be sexual creatures but Satan tries to pervert that natural desire and use it to achieve his goals to destroy families and individuals. God can help, and does, when we ask Him too. "Submit yourselves, then, to God. Resist the devil, and he will flee from you" (James 4:7). But that's the toughest part, submitting to God. We know in our hearts when we are about to do something we shouldn't. We can feel the anxiety built as we allow ourselves to continue to mull over the desire to act on the urge we are feeling. If we can muster the strength to ask God right then to help, He does. I know. . .

17 CONFLICT

Dealing with conflict is a necessity to maintain healthy relationships. Unfortunately, many people lack conflict management skills. With the divorce rate in America at approximately 50 percent, many children do not have good role models for resolving conflict. They live in homes of perpetual conflict. They see that the strongest, or loudest, or most powerful person usually gets their way. Teaching children good conflict management skills starts with parents being good role models.

Churches also have trouble with conflict resolution. Many churches break apart because individual members and church leaders lack the skills to keep a situation from getting out of hand. People are afraid to state the obvious, an opinion, or idea, because it might cause problems. But the real problems come when everyone remains quiet, or starts talking (gossips) about someone or to the wrong people. Churches should be able to help those that attend their services in dealing with conflict. Church leaders must also take an active role in heading off disputes before they fester into something that becomes uncontrollable.

Conflict is something everyone must deal with on a daily basis. For most, it comes in the form of routine decision making such as developing a schedule of daily activities, dealing with family situations, or possibly a conflict with work and family priorities. Most people can deal with these types of conflict with relative ease. They have resources at their disposal to readily handle these minor conflicts and minimize the stress related to these situations. For some though, conflict is much more imposing.

Even when a person is skilled at conflict resolution, they may try to avoid it if they sense possible danger in a confrontation. For example, if a woman lives with an abusive husband or even leaves the abusive situation, but must still deal with her estranged spouse, she may try to avoid any confrontation with him for fear of retribution. This poses a problem when minor children are involved for two obvious reasons for sure: She may give into unreasonable custody requests or not challenge unfair support or property settlements. Both, inevitably, end up hurting her and the children more than dealing with the conflict.

When a teacher sends a child home from school to abusive parents, or a co-worker is afraid to report fraud, waste or abuse, or a member of clergy covers up for another, because of possible retaliation, this just compounds the problem and prolongs the conflict. Wherever there is conflict, there is the possibility of danger to those involved regardless of how the situation is dealt with, including not dealing with it.

Ken Sande discusses three basic ways people deal with conflict: Escape, Attack, and Conciliation. The first two responses include denial and flight or litigation, assault, and/or murder respectively. Conciliation, on the other hand, involves several different options: overlooking the offense, discussion, negotiation, mediation, arbitration, or church discipline. It is possible to exercise these options privately, but when possible danger to another is a concern, a mediator is necessary.[1]

Coping with conflict in a healthy manner not only can

resolve a conflict but may also be an opportunity for change and growth and also to reflect God's power in relationships. Matthew 5:16 says, "In the same way, let your light shine before men, that they may see your good deeds and praise your Father in heaven." When we go to God to help us deal with conflict, He gives us a peace that passes all understanding. God's way is usually not the world's way, but He's always right! When we yield in this way, others see the outcome and God is glorified, but we must be willing to yield or that Light won't shine.

Dr. James Mallory says, "Anybody that is conflict free is not experiencing growth. . . the important changes in us take place within the framework of the struggle."[2] Jesus, Paul and many others emphasize this many times in the New Testament. If we don't have to deal with conflict, temptation, and the struggles of life in general, we do not grow in our relationship with the Lord or others. Christians should view conflict as an opportunity to grow and not view trials and adversity as the result of an uncaring, unfeeling God.

Five Approaches to Dealing With Conflict

Lowery and Myers discuss five approaches to dealing with conflict: avoidance, accommodation, competition, compromise, and collaboration.[3] The method used depends, a great deal, on the parties involved in the conflict. Are they bringing a cooperative or competitive attitude to the table, are they looking at the problem as an individual (independent) problem or is the problem perceived as a group (interdependent) problem? Another consideration is the amount of concern parties show for themselves and others; to what extent does each party intend on going to satisfy their own goals. Each approach may be a consideration for conflict resolution depending on the circumstances; however, collaboration is always the best solution when possible.

The first approach is avoidance. This approach is usually a poor choice because avoiding a problem does not make it go away. It usually intensifies the problem over time. Many people take the "No harm no foul" attitude when a problem seems minor. This may work on occasion but many times ignoring or avoiding the problem usually means a bigger problem at a later time. If dealt with immediately, small problems can remain small and easier to deal with. This approach indicates little concern for self or others.

Accommodation is characterized by a high concern for preserving a relationship, even if it means conceding one's own goals. The irony is, especially in marital relationships, that the person that concedes to keep peace in the relationship, thinking this is what will keep a relationship intact, is the person that is always conceding. They generally continue to give in during conflict and even begin to accept blame for the conflict and are blind to the selfishness of their spouse. When this is typical in a relationship, one person in the relationship is always giving and the other is always taking.

The taker is generally the cause of much of the conflict, because of their selfishness. The taker uses this to their advantage, knowing that their spouse will do anything it takes to avoid conflict and make them happy. When the taker doesn't get their way, they blame the giver for causing the conflict. This type of a response is typical in alcoholic homes. Those around the alcoholic do whatever is necessary to keep the peace and avoid conflict. It may also indicate a high need for acceptance by the giver. They send a message to the taker that their own needs are unimportant opening themselves up to the exploitation.

At times, this may be an appropriate response. If a person finds himself or herself facing a weapon or dealing with a hysterical person, they would be wise to accommodate the wishes of the person to defuse the situation. But generally speaking, most of the time this response sends a clear message to the other person involved in the conflict: Your needs are more important than mine and I'll do whatever it takes to make you happy. This will only lead to more conflict as the taker ups the ante and demands even more.

Competition is a win-or-lose style of conflict management, characterized by a very high achievement of personal goals, with little regard for the relationship. This can be a very high price to pay, especially in a personal relationship. This isn't always a face-to-face competition. Sometimes the combatants work subversively by misinformation, talking to others behind their counterparts back in an attempt to sway attitudes or in some way undermine the integrity of their foe. They may also use position power to gain control over a situation when other covert tactics fail.

Competition can be healthy and entertaining when it doesn't concern a serious matter. It may also be necessary when there is conflict involving personal values, especially if those values are biblically based. There's no room for compromising biblical principles.

Compromise involves searching out the middle ground for both or all parties involved. It is a medium concern for self and others and generally involves sharing. One side or the other is looking to make concessions and expect the same in return. Compromise is good when both parties gain ground in achieving their goal but can have negative connotations if integrity is lost in the process. This can lead to future conflicts and if one party or the other feels like they gave up more than the other there may be a lack of commitment in keeping the peace and staying on track.

Compromise is effective and very appropriate in certain situations. Federal and state legislators use compromise to achieve their objectives. Bills are passed or rejected based on a bartering system of give and take. Labor negotiations are another area where compromise is very appropriate. Again, whether workers strike or not depends on the agreements reached with management based on both parties' willingness to give and take.

The last approach to conflict resolution is collaboration. This is also the best approach to use. This approach indicates a high concern for all parties involved in a conflict: a win/win situation. When everyone involved with a conflict is committed to finding a mutually satisfying solution everybody wins. The collaborative style of conflict management can have many positive effects. When done consistently, it increases trust, builds stronger relationships, encourages enthusiastic goal implementation, and achieves a higher degree of conflict resolution just to name a few.

Jesus used several of these approaches to conflict management some time during His ministry. He avoided conflict when he retreated from the crowds; He accommodated everyone with His death on the cross. He used competition when discharging the money-changers from the temple. Though He used these techniques to deal with conflict, He never did at the expense of His integrity. We must also assure that we deal with conflict in a way that does not compromise our integrity so that we might be a godly example for those who seek our counsel.

When conflict remains unresolved

When conflict remains an issue and we find ourselves

dealing with constant stress, we look for ways to reduce the tension caused by the conflict. Most of the time people deal with this tension in healthy ways like finding someone to talk with, seeking counseling, exercising, or find some other means that provides relief without exacerbating the situation until it can be resolved. However, some resort to unhealthy remedies or quick fixes that only make matters worse. Self-satisfaction is a natural, albeit usually unhealthy way, to deal with stress because of how we try to satisfy ourselves, generally in ways that do not honor God.

CHOICES

18 GOD'S LOVE

On October 24th, 2002, I became a father for the third time. Each time one of my children was born, I felt an immediate love for them that I didn't think was humanly possible. From the moment I held each child for the first time, I felt an overwhelming love I didn't think myself capable of feeling. Indescribable joy filled my heart. How true the psalmist is when he says, "Sons are a heritage from the Lord, children a reward from him. Like arrows in the hands of a warrior are sons born in one's youth. Blessed is the man whose quiver is full of them" (Psalms 127:3-5). I would also add daughters to this passage.

When my first two children, Chelsea and Alex, were born, I was far away from the Lord. I still attended church occasionally, read my Bible once in a while, and prayed when I needed something. By some standards, this would qualify as being a good Christian. The problem was in my relationship with the Lord; I didn't seek His will for my life and I surly was not serving Him in any capacity at all. In fact, I was at a time in my life when I had all the answers, all you had to do was ask me and sometimes you didn't even have to do that, I just told you. The point is that I felt a love for my first two children I couldn't really explain, but I knew was very real.

Nearly twelve years after the birth of my son, I experienced that unexplainable love again with the birth of my second daughter Kori. At the time of her birth, as now, my relationship with the Lord is strong and growing stronger as time passes. Because of that strong relationship with God, I now understand that love I didn't know existed or thought possible until I became a father. That unconditional, agape love that I felt is the same love Jesus has for every human being!!!

This is the love Paul describes when he says, "Love is patient, love is kind. It does not envy, it does not boast, it is not proud. It is not rude, it is not self-seeking, it is not easily angered, and it keeps no record of wrongs. Love does not delight in evil but rejoices with the truth. It always protects, always trusts, always hopes, and always perseveres. Love never fails. But where there are prophecies, they will cease; where there are tongues, they will be stilled; where there is knowledge, it will pass away. For we know in part and we prophesy in part, but when perfection comes, the imperfect disappears. When I was a child, I talked like a child, I thought like a child, I reasoned like a child. When I became a man, I put childish ways behind me. Now we see but a poor reflection as in a mirror; then we shall see face to face. Now I know in part; then I shall know fully, even as I am fully known. And now these three remain; faith, hope and love. But the greatest of these is love" (1 Corinthians 13:4-13).

I have read this scripture passage countless times and I always envied those who were capable of this kind of love. Not until the birth of my third child did I realize that this is what I felt for all my children. More importantly, I realized and felt, for the first time how much God loves me and how much pain God endured watching His only Son die on the cross so that I may be reconciled to Him! He also endures that kind of pain when He watches us make poor choices and suffer the consequences of those choices because we didn't ask Him for guidance.

As I hug my children and pray for their health, knowing in my heart I only want what's best for them, I think of God embracing me and know that He only wants the best for me. There are times I wish I could somehow take on the pain and suffering my children must endure as part of life, so they don't have to feel pain. But character develops during difficult times. Pain, neither physical nor emotional, is pleasant and we may never understand why certain things happen that cause us pain, but in the end, when we trust God, we are stronger for the experience. But isn't that precisely what Jesus did when He died on the cross for our sins? How could a sinless man deserve such a fate? He didn't. Just as we intercede on behave of those we love, that's what Jesus did for us. How do you explain it except to say He did it for love?

The simplest of tasks that we do everyday can bring things to light when we are actively seeking the Lord's will in our life. This all occurred to me when I had to take my infant daughter in for her first round of childhood inoculations. As we arrived at the doctor's office, she was completely oblivious to why she was there, but I knew that she was there to get her shots. I also remember thinking I wish there was some way that they could stick me so she wouldn't have to feel the pain.

As I undressed her so the doctor could examine her, she was smiling and cooing completely unaware of what was about to happen, but I knew. I didn't want her to get stuck four times in the leg having no idea what was happening to her, but I also knew that it was better for her to suffer a little discomfort now versus fighting the effects of a life threatening disease later. I found no solace in this thought, but I knew it was best for her.

I found myself wondering, at this point, how often the

Lord had to make the same decision as far as I was concerned. How many times did the Lord have to endure watching me suffer through the trials of life, knowing that I'd be better for it in the end? Sometimes I may have been suffering as a result of my own selfish choices while other times it may be something I had absolutely no control over at all. Regardless of the circumstances, God feels the same pain for me, and for all of His children, that I feel for mine! "And so Jesus also suffered outside the city gate to make the people holy through his own blood" (Hebrews 13:12).

God wants us to call Him Father. Jesus teaches us that. That's the kind of relationship He wants to have with us if we are willing to let Him, and, like any good parent, He suffers when we suffer. God loves us all more than we can ever imagine. It is true that some things happen in our lives that we don't understand or don't see coming, but God does. Nothing gets by Him, if it happens; He allowed it to happen for a reason. I often wonder if God will give us the answers to some of those tough questions or unexplainable situations when we get to heaven, then I think, when I get to heaven will it really matter?

19 GOD WANTS ME?

When people come to the point in their life when they either accept or reject Christ, many wonder if God would even accept them if they did ask Him to. Countless times, as I've talked to individuals about the salvation God offers everyone through Jesus, I hear the question, "How could God want me as part of the family?" People often make statements like, I've hurt so many people; God could never forgive me; or I'd mess up the whole kingdom. The great news is God wants everyone regardless of their past!

This is very difficult for many people, including some Christians, to accept. Many feel that there are sins that are unforgivable, but that is the difference between God and us. We are the ones that have a problem with forgiveness, not Him. It is hard to imagine that God would allow someone who committed a horrible crime like rape or murder go to heaven, but you don't have to search the scriptures for long to find many examples of this happening.

David immediately comes to mind. He committed adultery with Bathsheba then abused his power as king by ordering the death of her husband Uriah. To make matters worse, the Bible tells us of how devoted Uriah was to both his wife and his king. David had Uriah brought back from the war with the Ammonites so he could sleep with his wife so her pregnancy would not implicate David. Uriah stayed at the palace because of his loyalty to the king and to the other soldiers. He said there was no way he could go home and enjoy all its comforts including the attention of his wife while everyone else was still in the middle of a battle.

It's probably safe to assume this caused David to feel even more guilt even though the Bible doesn't specifically address this. So David got Uriah drunk to try and encourage him to go home and sleep with his wife, but to no avail. One sin begat another and soon David found himself entangled in a web of lies. This is a man the Bible says was a man after God's own heart. Is this a statement about God's character? Yes it is! Not that God condones this type of behavior, but that He is forgiving of those who love Him.

He knew David's heart, and once confronted about his sin by Nathan, David confessed his sin and asked for forgiveness. David still suffered the consequences of his sin, but God forgave him. David yearned to be close to God and God knew that, but no matter how close our relationship with God, we can fall into sin. Covering it up only makes it worse as illustrated in David's story. God gave David many opportunities to repent, but he didn't until confronted by someone else. That's why the Bible tells us that when a brother is caught up in sin to rebuke him gently that he may recognize his sin.

It is very easy to get entangled in sin. Satan is very subtle about leading us into temptation. If we don't continue to put on the Armor of God to protect us from his schemes, we can find ourselves in a quagmire of sin before we know it. Covering it up only exacerbates the situation. Cyril Barber states, "Sin persistently followed, hardens the heart, deadens the conscience, atrophies faith and plunges the sinner to ever increasing depths so repentance becomes impossible, except by a miracle of God's Grace." Nathan was David's miracle. God used him to bring David to his senses and his knees: God forgave everything he did!

Jesus' life exemplifies forgiveness. I'm sure Jesus found many of the experiences He had with His disciples to be humorous if not hilarious but there were also several occasions when He experienced disappointment because of their actions. Peter is a good example of both extremes.

To say Peter was impetuous is an understatement. Peter is a classic example of the ready-fire-aim mentality. Peter was always speaking before thinking. But it's that same personality that compelled Peter to step out in faith at times when others wouldn't. His life was as much of a spiritual roller coaster as anyone past or present. Some of the highlights, and lowlights, were his selection by Jesus to be a disciple, being called Satan by Jesus, walking on water, and denying Christ.

Imagine the feeling of being personally selected by Jesus to be a disciple. He witnessed Jesus performing great miracles including healing his mother-in-law. He was there when Jesus fed over five thousand people with two fish and five loaves of bread. He was the first to profess Jesus as the Christ of God. He witnessed demons being cast out of people and watched as Jesus calmed a raging storm at sea while he himself was standing on the water with Jesus. What an incredible lesson in faith! I can't imagine the courage it took for Peter to step out of that boat onto the water to meet the Lord. But as soon as Peter started focusing on his circumstances instead of Jesus, he began to sink and cried out to Jesus to save him. How true of so many people, including myself. We have to be sinking in our circumstances before we cry out to Christ to save us.

After all these events the Bible tells us that Jesus called Peter, Satan! Peter took him aside and began to rebuke him. "Never, Lord!" he said. "This shall never happen to you!"

Jesus turned and said to Peter, "Get behind me, Satan! You are a stumbling block to me; you do not have in mind the things of God, but the things of men" (Matthew 16:22-23). Peter was thinking only of himself instead of the reason Jesus came to live among us: to save us. He couldn't imagine living without Jesus and was upset at the thought of His death.

Shortly before Jesus' arrest, Peter witnessed the transfiguration and promised Jesus he would rather die than deny Him. A few days later, Peter denied knowing Jesus, not just once, but three times, when Jesus was arrested. After His resurrection, Peter was one of the first to see Jesus. But later we find that even Paul referred to Peter as a hypocrite. "When Peter came to Antioch, I opposed him to his face, because he was clearly in the wrong. Before certain men came from James, he used to eat with the Gentiles. But when they arrived, he began to draw back and separate himself from the Gentiles, because he was afraid of those who belonged to the circumcision group. The other Jews joined him in his hypocrisy, so that by their hypocrisy even Barnabas was led astray" (Galatians 2:11-13).

After acknowledging Jesus as the Christ, Jesus blesses Peter. Jesus replied, "Blessed are you, Simon son of Jonah, for this was not revealed to you by man, but by my Father in heaven. And I tell you that you are Peter, and on this rock I will build my church, and the gates of Hades will not overcome it" (Matthew 16:17-18). It was just prior to Jesus rebuking Peter because of Satanic influences in his life that He tells Peter he would be the rock foundation for His church. Peter goes on to be one of the most outspoken apostles in spreading the gospel, standing up to the religious leaders of the day, healing people, and even raising the dead in Christ's name. Tradition tells us that Peter and Paul were likely martyred during the same period, A.D. 64 by the Roman Emperor Nero. Paul is another unlikely pillar of faith.

Paul, known as Saul before his conversion, killed Christians for a living. He was a murderer of those that loved Jesus! As Paul, he evangelized the world. He is arguably the greatest influence on Christians in history other than Jesus Himself. God wants us all regardless of our past. No matter your circumstances, past or present, He wants you, He loves you, and when you come to your senses, as the prodigal son did, He will run to you.

When or where does sin begin? We are born with a sin nature. The Bible makes it clear that all have sinned. Adam and Eve didn't sin until they disobeyed God and when they did, they knew it. They tried to hide themselves. Just as I mentioned in the chapter on personal responsibility quoting Jay Adams, we are not victims of our conscience; we are violators of it.

God instills in us a sense of right and wrong and gives us the Ten Commandments as a mirror for us to look into when we begin to feel self-righteous. We all sin despite our best efforts not to but God is quick to forgive if we are quick to confess. We still must deal with the consequences of our choices but we are forgiven. There is one sin however that God will not forgive: denying and rejecting Jesus. When we reject Him, we are eternally separated from the presence of the Lord. God wants us all to come to Him, that's why He sent Jesus to die for us. There's one catch: we have to ask Him for forgiveness and to save us from our sins. He won't force Himself on us, but He stands at the door knocking. Will you invite Him in or spend an eternity wishing you had? The choice is yours. . .

A Constant Struggle

Becoming a Christian doesn't mean you won't have to

deal with temptation and sin anymore. In fact, becoming a Christian is the beginning of a growing process that will test your faith. As we grow closer to God, we realize how far we are from where we need to be morally and spiritually. Our sin nature seems magnified when we compare our attitudes and actions with Jesus instead of those around us. We become acutely aware of how much temptation is around us and how easy and often we give into it.

Paul talks about this in his letter to the Romans when he speaks of his own struggle. He sums up how we all feel when he said; "I know that nothing good lives in me, that is, in my sinful nature. For I have the desire to do what is good, but I cannot carry it out. For what I do is not the good I want to do; no, the evil I do not want to do--this I keep on doing. Now if I do what I do not want to do, it is no longer I who do it, but it is sin living in me that does it.

"So I find this law at work: When I want to do good, evil is right there with me. For in my inner being I delight in God's law; but I see another law at work in the members of my body, waging war against the law of my mind and making me a prisoner of the law of sin at work within my members. What a wretched man I am! Who will rescue me from this body of death" (Romans. 7:18-24)?

We all have weaknesses but God uses our weaknesses for His glory. In fact God tells us, "My grace is sufficient for you, for my power is made perfect in weakness" (2 Corinthians 12:9). When we struggle we can't get down on ourselves. That's exactly what Satan wants us to do. He wants us to think we might as well quit trying, there's no point, and we're worthless. He knows he's lost the battle for our soul when we ask Christ into our hearts, but if he can discourage us enough, he doesn't have to worry about us influencing others to accept Christ. When that happens, he wins!

We must always remember we will struggle with our faith and with temptation because this is not a battle of flesh and blood but a spiritual battle being fought in high places. We will have moments of weakness but it is at those moments that we need to call on Jesus to help us overcome, to fight our battles, the battles only He can fight and win. When we are weak, He is strong. All the heroes of the Bible had weaknesses that God used to His glory. We can use our weaknesses as excuses to not get involved in serving the Lord, rationalizing that we would only hurt the cause or we can roll up our sleeves, get involved and trust the Lord. The more we trust Him, the less we struggle.

CHOICES

SUMMARY

Mankind considers Christianity a religion along with the countless other religions of the world. Unfortunately many followers of Christianity end up following religious guidelines devised by men that only distort the truth and cause people to fall away from Christ. It sours them to the point that they have no desire to get to know Christ. In many cases it's very understandable but tragic at the same time. They may never come to know Christ because of the treatment they receive from people claiming to be Christians. Satan is the great deceiver and it is not beyond him to use the church to create confusion; in fact, it's one of his favorite schemes.

Religion puts God in a box, or should I say, puts us in a box, that limits God's ability to work in our lives because of our reluctance to allow Him to. Religion tells us what we can't do; God tells us what we can. He tells us in His word that He came that we might have life and have it more abundantly, but that's only possible when we ask Him into our hearts to be the Lord of our life.

Jesus doesn't expect us to meet certain prerequisites before we can ask Him to be the Lord of our lives. If that were the case, He would never have come to die for us. He came while we were still sinners to set us free, "God demonstrates his own love for us in this: While we were still sinners, Christ died for us" (Romans 5:8). He wants us just as we are!

He makes the changes in our lives as He sees fit to do. We just need to trust Him; but so many people just can't seem to take that first step.

If Jesus lived in our society today, He would be considered an uneducated, homeless man that preferred the company of beggars and thieves to that of those in the religious community. But that shouldn't be surprising, because that is how He was treated 2,000 years ago. How much attention or credibility would He receive? None. He would be looked at as just another religious lunatic. Fortunately for us, we have history on our side. We can look back through time and know He is who He said He is.

The church should be a place that people can go to learn more about Jesus and how much He loves us and a place of support and comfort, not a place where they receive judgment and ridicule. As people learn to look at God outside of the box religion places Him in, they learn about an incredibly loving, gracious, and forgiving God, that longs to have an intimate, personal relationship with them. They learn that He is not a God that sits on high waiting to dole out punishment on unbelievers. He wants to interact with us, rejoice and laugh with us, celebrate life with us. His desire is that nobody perish, that everyone would come to Him. When we read His word and become closer to Him through prayer and service, we learn that we don't have to give up anything, even though he gave up everything. We gain considerably, not the way the world looks at gain, but as God does. We learn that God doesn't restrict. Quite the contrary, He sets us free.

Jesus expects the church to be an extension of Him. But how can it be when we try to add to the instructions found in His word? But isn't that the crux of the matter anyway? Don't we often feel that we know what's better for us rather than trusting that God knows what He's doing as far as we're concerned? We can lay anything, including our lives, at His feet, but He won't do anything unless we are willing to leave it there. It's not that He can't mind you, but He loves us so much, He won't force Himself on us. We must choose.

To be a Christian is to be Christ-like. How can we do that without knowing who He is? If we aspire to be like anyone, we must first know that person in order to be like him or her. The same is true of being like Jesus. We must know Him. When we do, He provides for all our needs. Jesus told the woman at the well that He would give her Living Water so that she would never thirst again. That emptiness that we all feel inside at one time or another in our lives is that thirst that only Jesus can quench. We try to fill it with sex, drugs, money, charity, and religion just to name a few, but what we really thirst for is something only Christ can offer: Living Water. It is the only thing that satisfies that thirst, and a personal relationship with Jesus is the only way to drink of that Living Water.

From a personal point of view, I can say that the water Christ provides is ultimately refreshing! To know Jesus and to have a personal relationship with Him are entirely different. Satan knows Jesus, he believes in God, just like many people do, but that won't get him into heaven. We must turn our life over to Him and yield to His will. Pride prevents many from taking that step of faith. That was the cause of Satan's fall: his pride.

Once I decided to trust the Lord with all of my heart, to yield to His will, He has kept my paths straight. Until then, He patiently waited for me, keeping a hedge around me to protect me from many things, especially myself. As I continue to seek His will in my life, it becomes easier to trust

Him. I knew Him for years but trusted myself and my life was a series of disasters. Now I look forward to what's ahead.

That's not to say that I still don't have times of trouble and suffering. I live in a fallen world with people that still believe in looking out only for themselves. I can say that when times of trouble come, I have a source of strength that sustains me, and a peace that truly surpasses all understanding. Jesus stood at the door of my heart and knocked for years. I invited Him in as a small child but did not learn to trust Him until I began to trust Him as a child trusts his father. He wants us to call Him Father; He allows us the opportunity to choose. What will your choice be? He's waiting.

EPILOGUE

In closing, I would like to make one thing very clear. When I talk about taking God out of the box, I'm not suggesting that we reinvent God by changing scripture to say what is convenient for us, so we can live our lives as we please, but still claim to love and follow God. God's word is very clear on the consequences of doing that. Nor do I want, in any way, to question His deity and majesty. Quite the contrary, what I'm suggesting is that we search the scriptures, in a prayerful way, asking the Lord to reveal to us who He is and what His will is for our life. We should not accept someone's word about who He is or what He expects of us, but to find the answers for ourselves. I must admit, it is not an easy task but it is well worth the effort.

I believe the Bible is God's Holy Word and all Scripture is God breathed. Just as God used men and women like Abraham, Noah, Moses, David, Job, Solomon, Ruth, Mary, and countless others to instruct His people and pave the way for Jesus' arrival, He used men and women to compose and collate the Bible. I'm sure compiling sixty-six books of selected writings into a set of instructions for humanity is not to big a task for the Creator of the universe. Everything we need to know about God, human nature, and dealing with the trials and joys of life can be found within its covers if we are only willing to look. There is a caveat to this however. The Bible also makes it very clear that without accepting Jesus as our personal Lord and Savior, we will think His word is nonsense.

But that is the point. For years and years I was told what the Bible said. Most of what I learned was true; however, there were also many things that weren't biblical at all. They were man-made rules based on poor interpretations or personal convictions that had nothing to do with what God's word said. So many people turn away or never come to know Jesus because of religion. They turn away from the gospel. The Bible also makes it clear that teachers and preachers of the word will be held accountable for how they present God's word to the world.

Dr. Scott Teutsch is the senior pastor at Eastwood Baptist Church in Northwest Louisiana. He has been a good friend and mentor for many years now. He is one of the most knowledgeable people I know regarding the Bible. He is also an outstanding teacher of the word. He has an incredible knack for applying scripture, including Old Testament writings, to our culture and life in the 21st century.

One of the characteristics about his teaching style I most admire is, even though he is a very learned man and excellent teacher of the word; he remains very humble. He challenges everyone that hears him preach and teach God's word to search their hearts and the scriptures so they may be sure he is speaking the truth based on God's word and not Scott's interpretation of God's word. As I'm sure he'd testify, I've challenged him on more than one occasion.

Those challenges, based on my reading scripture and praying about what I've read and what it means to me personally, are just some of the ways that I've increased my knowledge about, and relationship, with Jesus. Reading countless other Christian authors contributed to my knowledge base, as did the counsel of many wonderful Christian men and women. That is the reason fellowship is so important; that we can continue to grow in Christ. Churches should be an extension of Christ. That is only possible when the church actively seeks and teaches the truth. Each of us, individually seeking a personal relationship with Jesus, accomplishes that one person at a time.

I've always been a show me kind of person. That's one reason I had such a hard time yielding my life to Christ. My search for understanding about God's word revealed that many people struggled with the same problem I did. I also discovered that there are very well known pastors out there, pastoring very large congregations, that feel much the same way I do about how people treat others in the name of Jesus. I found this to be very encouraging. However the greatest evidence I found of God's power and love did not come from the wisdom of others but from seeing He still works in and through those who believe and trust in Him: seeing lives changed!

I'd like to close with a quote from the personal devotion book *Our Daily Bread*. In a piece dated 13 April 2003 titled The King's Offer, the author writes, "Many Jews failed to recognize that before Jesus would openly assert His sovereignty He had to rule in their hearts. Their greatest need was not to be freed from Caesar's rule but to be released from the chains of pride, self-righteousness, and rebellion against God." [1]

That is my challenge to you, Seek the Lord with all your heart, mind, and soul. Break down the religious paradigms that form barriers between you and Jesus. Martin Luther King said, "the truth shall set us free." Jesus is the truth and he wants to set you free, He's just waiting for you to knock. I know every excuse there is to not become a Christian and not attend church. I've tried to address many of them in this book, including the issue of those pesky hypocrites. Just remember we're all sinners and Jesus is the only way to rectify the sin issue and reconcile us to God. If your question is how do I get to heaven, Jesus answered, "I am the way and the truth and the life. No one comes to the Father except through me" (John 14:6). It's an eternal choice...what will your choice be?

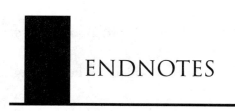

ENDNOTES

Chapter 4
1. *The Question of God.* Dr. Armand M. Nicholi, Jr. The Free Press, 2002.

Chapter 6
1. *The Purpose Driven Life.* Rick Warren, Zondervan Publishing. 2002.

Chapter 7
1. *The Purpose Driven Life.* Rick Warren, Zondervan Publishing. 2002.

Chapter 8
1. *The Purpose Driven Life.* Rick Warren, Zondervan Publishing. 2002.

Chapter 11
1. *Competent to Counsel.* Jay E. Adams. Zondervan Publishing House. 1970.

Chapter 14
1. *The Road Less Traveled.* M. Scott Peck, M.D. Simon and Schuster. 1978.
2. *Mind Games.* Andre Kole and Jerry MacGregor. Harvest House Publishers. 1998.

Chapter 15
1. *Prayer and You.* Cecil G. Osborne, Word Books, 1974. (Not previously listed.)
2. *The Case of Faith.* Lee Strobel. Zondervan Publishing. 2000.
3. *He Came to Set The Captives Free.* Rebecca Brown, M.D. Whitaker House. 1992.

Chapter 17
1. *The Peacemaker.* 2nd Edition. Ken Sande. Baker Books. 1997.
2. *The Kink and I.* James Mallory and S. Baldwin. Wheaton, Ill., Victor Books. 1973.
3. Lowery and Myers. 1991.

Epilogue
1. *Our Daily Bread.* RBC Ministries. 2002.

* All Scripture passages are from the *Life Application Study Bible*. (NIV) Tyndale House Publishers & Zondervan Publishing House. 1997.

PERSONAL PROFILE

Thomas C. Saunders Jr. was born on September 9, 1958 in Flint Michigan, the first of six siblings. He graduated from Elizabeth Ann Johnson Memorial High School in Mt. Morris, Michigan in June 1976. He joined the United States Air Force in February 1977. After completing basic training in Texas, he received training as an aircraft weapons specialist in Denver Colorado. Upon completion of technical school he transferred to central California for two years before moving on to Torrejon Air Base in Madrid Spain.

He separated from the Air Force in May of 1981 and worked in Ohio as a business machine repairman. He rejoined the Air Force in November of 1982 transferred to a base in Northern Lower Michigan. In May of 1986 he moved to Northwest Louisiana where he stayed until his retirement from the military in May 1999. From July 1997 to July 1998 he did a remote tour of duty at Kunsan Air Base, Republic of Korea (South Korea). There he served as a lay minister and served in many other capacities at the base chapel.

While stationed in Louisiana he completed his education and began teaching college for the Community College of the Air Force (CCAF) and Bossier Parish Community College in Northwest Louisiana. He has two Associate of Applied Science degrees from CCAF, one in Aircraft Weapons Systems Technology and one as an Instructor of

Technology and Military Science. He has a Bachelor of Science in Industrial Technology from Southern Illinois College of Engineering and Technology, a Master of Arts from Louisiana Tech in Human Relations Management and Supervision and a Ph.D. in Psychology and Christian Counseling from Louisiana Baptist University.

Tom is married to Lauri Ann (LaFave) Saunders of Harper Woods Michigan. They have three children, Chelsea Lorrayne Saunders (16) and Alexander Christian Saunders (12) who reside with their mother in Benton, Louisiana and Kori Alexis Saunders age 8 months. They enjoy any outdoor activity and they are members of Colonial Hills Baptist Church in Mt. Morris, Michigan.